Born In 1973

How Times Have Changed

Elizabeth Absalom & Malcolm Watson

D'AZUR PUBLISHING

BORN IN 1973
HOW TIMES HAVE CHANGED

Published by D'Azur Publishing 2022
D'Azur Publishing is a Division of D'Azur Limited

First published in Great Britain in 2022 by D'Azur Limited
Contact: info@d-azur.com Visit www.d-azur.com
3rd Edition Published 2023
ISBN 9798371859150

ACKNOWLEDGEMENTS
The publisher wishes to acknowledge the following people and sources:

British Newspaper Archive; The Times Archive; p5 Rico Shen; p7 Eddi Laumanns; p11 Malcolm Watson; p13 The Royal Mint Museum; p13 MaundyMoney.info; p13 GB Classic Coins ; p15 Honerarchive.com; p15 Pasttenseblog; p17 National Museum of American History; p17 Spy Musuem; p19 The Advertising Cliché; p25 Sixties City; p29 Stephen Thomas; p29 John F. Mailer. Canada. National Film Board of Canada. Library and Archives Canada; p30 MacDonalds; p38 Vintage Dancer; p44 Science Museum; p44 JodyKingzett; p45 NASA; P45 Salvatore Barbera; p49 Eduard Marmet airliners.net; p51 Wadhurst History Society; p66 Atreyu own work; p66 David Merrett; p67 YouTube; p69 Cédric Janodet; p69 Ken Fielding; p75 Juan Solis; p81 Ethical Trekkin; p81 davidoffnorthide; p85 Corporate Finance Institute; p87 Kingkongphoto; p82 This file is licensed under the Creative Commons Attribution 2.5 Generic license; p95 The Step Blog; p99 Klaviyo; p99 Freshexchange.com; p100 Netflix; p101 Alex Needham ; p101 Willie Duggan ; p103 Dan Heap ; p103 Sergeant Rupert Frere; p104 Dave Comeau; p105 John Douglas ; p108 Hair and makeup Artists Handbook; Rare Historical Photos; p110 Hagerty.co.uk; PistonHeads; Theteslachannel.com; p111 wish.com; ebaumsworld.com; p112 BMJ; Gillings School of Global Public Health; p113 Nike; p119 McDonalds; Office for National Statistics; Burger King; p120 The Furniture Market; p121 Fatsoma;

Whilst we have made every effort to contact copyright holders, should we have made any omission, please contact us so that we can make the appropriate acknowledgement.

CONTENTS

LIFE IN

Monarch: Queen Elizabeth II

Prime Minister: Edward Heath, Conservative Party

In 1973, Edward Heath was presiding over another year which was brought to a halt by industrial action, a period of falling productivity and inflation. His government was embroiled in curbing trade union power and the country was beset with striking British workers in all walks of life. There was the oil crisis and a three-day-week set to begin on the last day of the year. Britain joined the EEC; the IRA extended their bloody havoc to the mainland and bombed London whilst the Northern Irish referendum voted to remain part of the UK.

The US ended its involvement in the Vietnam War; we had cod wars with Iceland; the first episode of 'Last of the Summer Wine'; Little Jimmy Osmond reached No1 with 'Long Haired Lover from Liverpool'; David Bowie retired his Ziggy Stardust persona and Roger Moore played his first Bond in 'Live And Let Die'.

FAMOUS PEOPLE WHO WERE BORN IN 1973

Apr 5th: Pharrell Williams, American singer
Apr 24th: Lee Westwood, English golfer
Jun 25th: Jamie Redknapp, English footballer
Jul 2nd: Peter Kay, English Comedian
Jul 23rd: Monica Lewinsky, White House Intern
Jul 26th: Kate Beckinsale, English Actress
Sep 29th: Alfie Boe, English tenor
Dec 17th: Paula Radcliffe, English Athlete
Dec 18th: Lucy Worsley, English Historian

FAMOUS PEOPLE WHO DIED IN 1973

Jan 22nd: Lyndon B Johnson, US President
Jan 26th: Edward G Robinson, American actor
Mar 26th: Sir Noël Coward, English playwright
Apr 8th: Pablo Picasso, Spanish artist
Jun 30th: Nancy Mitford, English writer
Jul 2nd: Betty Grable, American actress
Jul 18th: Jack Hawkins, English actor
Sep 2nd: JRR Tolkien, British writer
Sep 29th: WH Auden, English poet

1973

In 1973 Value Added Tax at 10% replaced the old purchase tax and Surtax was removed, to be replaced by nine incremental rates of income tax, starting at 30% for less than £5,000 pa to the top rate of 75% for over £20,000 pa.

It seemed a golden age of television comedy, 'Continental quilts' were taking over from sheets and blankets and 'Baby Alive', the doll that could eat, drink, and even wet itself, one of the grossest toys ever made, was released!

The First Cell Phone

In 1973, there wasn't the Internet, digital cameras, or personal computers, but there was the cell phone. The prototype version that would become the Motorola DynaTAC 8000x weighed 2.5 pounds, and had a single-line, text-only LED screen. It took a decade before it finally reached consumer's hands

Our Favourite Foods

We entertained our friends with German sweet wines, Blue Nun and Black Tower and the new and exciting import from Europe, the Fondue party. We ate chilli con carne and spaghetti Bolognese, changing our familiar potatoes for rice and pasta.

How Much Did It Cost?

The Average Pay:	£38.10 per week
The Average House:	£9,000
Loaf of White Bread:	11½p
Pint of Milk:	5½p
Pint of Beer:	18½p
Dozen Eggs:	32p
Gallon of Petrol:	39p (7½p a litre)
Newspapers:	3p to 5p
To post a letter in UK:	3p 2nd , 3½p 1st class
TV Licence:	£7 B&W £12 Colour

JANUARY 1973

IN THE NEWS

WEEK 1

"Britain Joins the EEC" The United Kingdom, Ireland and Denmark become the newest members of the European Economic Community, bringing the total number of member states to nine.

"Compensation Offer Raised to £22m" The Distillers Company increased their offer to Britain's thalidomide children. If accepted, it means £2m a year for 10 years into a charitable trust fund to give an income to the estimated 410 victims.

WEEK 2

"Civil Service Protest at Freeze" Disruption and wide-spread stoppages in ministry and government departments was caused by Civil Service union leaders as a result of their call for 'work time meetings'.

"First Open University Degrees Awarded" The first graduates from the Open University (OU) have been awarded their degrees after two years studying from home. Out of the 1,000 students who sat the final exams, 867 were successful.

WEEK 3

"Heath's 3 Year Grip" The Government will keep strict controls on prices, pay, dividends and rent for the next three years. The TUC refuse their co-operation.

WEEK 4

"East End Tibbs Gang Jailed" Sentences amounted to 58 years for Tibbs, his 3 sons and associates after their reign of hatred, fear and terror in London.

"Nixon Announces Vietnam Peace" The US president, Richard Nixon, has announced "peace with honour" in Vietnam.

HERE IN BRITAIN

"Oh! Yes Calcutta"

The film version of the revue Oh! Calcutta! was recommended for exhibition in London. After viewing it for the second time, the chairman of the Greater London Council's film viewing subcommittee said, *"We decided this was a film that should be shown. We had a spirited minority and there is no doubt other members of the GLC will want to see it."*

Opinions ranged from, *"the funniest film. A 'nude romp', but nudity is not pornographic"*, to, *"Oh! Calcutta! is the most cruel, sadistic and sick piece of pornography of any kind I have ever seen, and I have seen everything".*

AROUND THE WORLD

"New York's Expectant Fathers"

Men's Lib is on the verge of a great victory in New York. The federal Equal Employment Opportunity Commission has agreed that male teachers should be given paternity leave when their wives have babies.

The baby which has provoked this revolutionary development, was born three years ago. Ever since, the father has been arguing that he should be allowed to take the same four years' unpaid leave from his teaching post that mothers are granted automatically. At the end of their four years, mothers can go back to their jobs with all their seniority and other privileges preserved for them.

Jean-Claude Andruet in the winning Renault Alpine

Renault announces the results of the Monte Carlo Rally because no one else wanted to.

1. Renault Alpine
2. Renault Alpine
3. Renault Alpine
4. Ford Escort
5. Renault Alpine
6. Renault Alpine
7. Fiat 124
8. Lancia
9. Datsun
10. Renault Alpine

The Monte Carlo Rally is the roughest kind of race. More than 3,000 miles of driving over all kinds of terrain. This year, more than 250 cars attempted to win at Monte Carlo but only one did. The Renault Alpine. First, second and third place and six finishers in the top ten. Which doesn't leave anyone else much to brag about.

We don't sell the Renault Alpine in this country. But we do sell the Renault 12,15 and 17. And each of these cars has a souped down version of the engine that won at Monte Carlo. Plus front-wheel drive, rack and pinion steering and a lot of other features the average American driver looks for. So if you're looking for a winner, come in and check out a Renault. If you're not, there are a lot of other cars to choose from.

Pat Moss-Carlsson

MUTINY AT THE MONTE RALLY

The Monte Carlo Rally turned into a mutiny on the final day when disqualified drivers blocked the route with cars. Likened to a "Keystone Cops" comedy, leading drivers ploughed across fields, through back gardens and along pavements to miss the hold up. Armed French police got caught up in the chaos as they tried to clear the way.

The row had begun the day before at Le Burzet, in the French Alps, after one car crashed during a speed test … and 144 more got stuck behind it in heavy snow. After a four and a half hour wait while bulldozers tried to clear a path all 144 crews were told, *"You're disqualified."* Thirty of the rebels took a short cut to Digne and blocked the road, but sixty drivers – including Britain's Pat Moss Carlsson – made hair-raising cross-country detours to get past. The furious rebels chased after them and there were scuffles in Monte Carlo as police escorted the leaders in. One of the British drivers who helped to block the rally route said, *"It was a b***** shambles. We found ourselves cut off from the rally and then after four hours a little office girl came up and told us we were eliminated."*

On the last day, 30 of the eliminated crews set out from Monaco and completely jammed the rally route, forcing the organizers to abandon the final phase. As surviving cars straggled back into Monaco by any route they fancied, the demonstrators gathered in front of the Automobile Club and formed a human wall across the road to stop cars reaching the final check point. Altogether about 120 cars were put out of the rally because of the blockage at Burzet. Among those who cut across country to avoid the demonstration was Rauno Aaltonen, he leapt over a ditch and burst through a hedge, narrowly missing a police car.

FEBRUARY 1973

IN THE NEWS

WEEK 1   **"Pan Am and TWA Will Not Buy Concorde"** America's two main international airlines announced they are cancelling their options to buy the Concorde.

WEEK 2   **"Protestant Mobs Rampage in Ulster"** Ulster loyalists attacked Roman Catholic homes and property in many parts of the province yesterday during a day of protest against the imprisonment, without trial, of two young Protestants.

         "Gas Workers Strike" There was a potential danger to millions of British homes as the gas workers' dispute begins began to take effect. Gas pressure was cut to homes and hundreds of firms lost supply.

WEEK 3   **"Vietnam Ceasefire Failure"** All four Vietnam military groups are blamed for the deplorable situation as fighting increases.

         "Teachers on Strike and Bookies Threaten" More than 40,000 children had the day off from 73 outer London schools and the Grand National could be without a bet.

WEEK 4   **"Jet Shot Down"** 74 people died when a Libyan airliner was brought down in the Sinai desert after being intercepted by Israeli fighters.

         "Black Box Shows Pilot Was Lost" The Israel defence forces announced that the black box of the Libyan airliner shot down by Israel fighters showed that the crew believed they were over Egypt and that the fighters circling round them were MiGs.

HERE IN BRITAIN
"Waste-Not Wombles"

The BBC introduced a television programme intended partly to make children aware of environmental pollution. The programmes are about hairy, mildly priggish, rat-like creatures called "Wombles" with a passion for tidiness and making good use of bad rubbish scattered by humans on Wimbledon common.
Wombles adapt human junk to furnish their burrows and call each other fancy names such as Tobermory, Orinoco, and Tomsk taken from an old, rubbishy atlas. Great Uncle Bulgaria and his family will be seen patching their roof with toffee papers and mending their rocking chair with old tyres with the anthem "Wombles are tidy and Wombles are clean."

AROUND THE WORLD
"US PoWs Arrive In Philippines"

In the Philippines, a colour guard, a red carpet and warm handshakes greeted the 143 American prisoners of war flown from Hanoi. There was a marked difference in attitude. For those from North Vietnam, looking worn and tired in their baggy blue and grey uniforms but maintaining rigid military discipline and those from Vietcong captivity with no trace of martial discipline, wearing grey-green pyjama-style clothes and sandals made of a tyre tread, wearing bamboo necklaces and one with a flower behind his ear. However, the overriding thought in all their minds was – ice-cream! "We've been thinking of ice cream for years."

In The News

1973
Water Ox

The Year Of The Ox

The Chinese New Year of the Ox began life with a big bang. Gerrard Street, Soho, the Chinatown of London, was thronged for their festival to celebrate the end of the Year of the Rat and the beginning of the Year of the Ox. Barrages of firecrackers imported from Hong Kong were let off in the car park at the end of the street, filling the afternoon with acrid gunpowder smoke and the shrieks of children. Every shop was festooned with red lanterns, scarlet banners and Chinese poems.

Fishing lines baited with strings of lettuce were dangled from upper windows for the lion of the traditional Chinese lion dance, a terrifying but herbivorous beast of many colours, who came dancing down the street, leaping and shaking his head in time to cymbals and drums. A lion-tamer in a round red mask guided him from lettuce to lettuce with a straw fan in each hand. The Loon Fung supermarket had pictures of the Ox of the year, a sleek beast descending some stairs, on show beside Peking red wine and boxes of shrimp chips. Every child entering the street was given a handful of sweets and a gas-filled balloon.

One of the distributors of sweets said that the essential point of Chinese New Year was that it should be a family reunion. *"There is no special food that we eat at new year, just an enormous lot of food."* When Gerrard Street began its history in the seventeenth century it was a military parade ground. The first Chinese restaurant was opened in 1926 and now almost every shop has become Chinese. From all the shops Chinese music tinkled, gongs sounded and the scents of fried prawn balls and honey barbecued pork ribs spiced the air and happy crowds surged along.

MARCH 1973

IN THE NEWS

WEEK 1   **"Week of Strikes"** Railway footplatemen, Gas workers, Fords and NHS non-medical staff. All taking industrial action this week.

"BEA Bans Flights Over France" Whilst the French Air Traffic Controllers were on strike, two Spanish airliners crashed in mid-air over France, killing 68 passengers and crew.

WEEK 2   **"Northern Ireland Votes for Union"** In a referendum on the future of the province, the people voted overwhelmingly to remain within the United Kingdom.

"British Officials Shot Dead in Bermuda" The British governor and his assistant were assassinated in Bermuda, a British-dependent territory in the North Atlantic.

"London Terror Bombs" One man died, and 238 people were injured when IRA bombs exploded in front of the Central Criminal Court and outside an Army recruiting office in Whitehall. Two other bombs at New Scotland Yard and in Westminster were defused.

WEEK 3   **"Gun Boat Causes Trawlers to Collide"** Two Grimsby trawlers were in collision as a result of harassment by the Icelandic gunboat Aegir in the north-sea 'cod wars'. The trawlers Arsenal and the Aldershot were damaged when trying to take avoiding action.

WEEK 4   **"Stock Exchange Admits Women"** Women have been admitted to the London Stock Exchange for the first time in the institution's 200-year history.

HERE IN BRITAIN
"Gears? What Gears?"

An American woman hired a little family saloon to drive from London to Bodmin. 240 miles but she used 54 gallons of petrol to get there. She had been warned British cars were different from 'those back home' but crawling along didn't seem right, and she eventually called for help.

"How are the gear changes?" asked the friendly AA man. "What gears" she asked looking at the gear lever firmly positioned in second, "I haven't touched them!" She was used only to automatic cars and manual gearboxes were a mystery to her, as is how she managed to start the car in the first place.

AROUND THE WORLD
"John Won't Leave Without Yoko"

America ordered former Beatle John Lennon out of the country because of previous drugs convictions in Britain. He and his Japanese born wife Yoko Ono issued a statement, *"Having just celebrated our fourth anniversary we are not prepared to sleep in separate beds. Peace and Love from John and Yoko."*

Making the decision to leave the States was agonising for Yoko as she had been given permission to stay permanently, to continue the search for Kyoko, her daughter from a previous marriage. She and Lennon were given custody of the nine-year-old by a Texas court last year but Kyoko and her British film-maker father, vanished.

The new, 1973, unimpressive, London Bridge.

The original London Bridge relocated to Arizona

Tower Bridge

The New London Bridge

Ten thousand people watched the Queen go walk-about on the new London Bridge and perform the official opening ceremony just eight days after the bomb outrages that brought terror to the Capital. With all the talk of security, it was left to the sunshine, the colourful aplomb of the City of London's pageantry and the Queen's arrival to turn minds to the matter in hand.

Her Majesty travelled by river launch from Westminster and landed at Fishmonger's Quay to a 41-gun salute by the Honourable Artillery Company at the Tower. She had twice sailed under the bridge.

After seeing a display depicting its history, she was welcomed on the dais by the Lord Mayor. The Queen said, "London Bridge may not be the longest, the tallest, or the widest bridge in the world, but I believe as you, do, that it is the most famous. It has played a vital part in the history and prosperity of this city and, like other great institutions, has passed into the folklore of the country. I am glad to report that it shows no signs of falling down, far from it, it is clearly here to stay." The bridge had been built, and the old one demolished, without the traffic flow across and beneath it ever being halted. "This has been a great achievement."

At the opening she met representatives of the McCulloch Oil Corporation of California, who bought the old bridge and re-erected it in the United States – allegedly believing it to be the rather more impressive 'Tower Bridge'. After unveiling a plaque, the Queen was presented with a gold medallion and a booklet describing the history of the bridges. About twenty of the people involved in the £5.5m project were presented to her and included three Irish labourers, one in morning dress.

APRIL 1973

IN THE NEWS

WEEK 1

"Unions Give Heath a Break" The miner's national strike is called off and the PM given a chance to fight inflation. Mortgages set to rise to 9½%.

"VAT introduced in Britain" The tax on goods and services was set at 10% and replaced the previous Purchase Tax.

WEEK 2

"Art Master Picasso Dies" The artist Pablo Picasso has died of a heart attack at his chateau near Cannes on the French Riviera.

"Day-Trip Britons Die" At least 100 Britons, the majority of them married women from four Somerset villages on a one-day charter flight to Switzerland, died when a Vanguard airliner crashed in a snowstorm south of Basel.

WEEK 3

"Picasso's Collection Bequeathed to the Louvre" His collection of modern paintings, probably the greatest private collection of work by the Spanish master's contemporaries, is to be given to France.

WEEK 4

"Iceland Patrol Boat Rammed" Twenty British trawlers, lined up like men-of-war, engaged Icelandic patrol boats in a night battle in the disputed fishing grounds. Two trawlers emerged spattered with rifle shots and a patrol boat and another trawler limped away with gashes after a collision.

"Nixon Takes Rap for Watergate Scandal" President Richard Nixon has taken full responsibility for the Watergate scandal but has denied any personal involvement.

HERE IN BRITAIN

"Post Office Raid"

A gang nicknamed the 'Tightrope Mob' blasted open a Post Office strongroom and escaped with £600,000. It is thought to be the biggest raid ever, but it's thought they panicked and an even richer prize was missed, possibly as much as £2m.

The gang earned their nickname by the way they got out of the Twickenham post office, they bridged the gap between a first-floor windowsill and a 12' high wire fence with a narrow plank. *"They must have been getting in some high wire practice. They needed nerves of steel to do that in the dark,"* said one detective.

AROUND THE WORLD

"Picasso Dies Aged 91"

Pablo Picasso, arguably the greatest painter of modern times, died this month at his home near Cannes. His local doctor said his heart had failed. The Spanish painter, probably the wealthiest artist who ever lived, had announced only a few days before that a Picasso festival was to be held this summer in the Palace of the Popes at Avignon where some 200 wash and brush paintings of his last years were to be shown.

Many of the paintings were of children and critics said they displayed a remarkable serenity. Posters reproducing a painting showing an artist with his brush poised had already gone out.

POLISHED SILVER MAUNDY MONEY

The distribution of Maundy Money, which takes place on the Thursday before Easter, is the modern development of an ancient ceremony said to be derived from when Christ washed his disciples' feet the evening before his crucifixion. In Britain the service goes back many centuries and Elizabeth I personally took part in 1572, in the hall at Greenwich. On that occasion a laundress, the sub-Almoner and the Lord High Almoner washed the feet of the poor people, and the feet then being, apparently, thoroughly clean, were again washed and kissed by the Queen herself. She then distributed broadcloth for the making of clothes and fish, bread and wine.

Royalty continued to take part but the last time the foot-washing ritual took place was in 1685. Several changes have taken place since then. Clothing was substituted for broadcloth for the women but that was stopped in 1724 and money was given in lieu. In 1837 William IV agreed to give the pensioners thirty shillings in lieu of all provisions.

For many years the ceremony took place in Whitehall Chapel moving later to Westminster Abbey. Today, the service is held in various cathedrals and the Queen, accompanied by the Duke of Edinburgh, has personally distributed her royal gift almost every year since her coronation. In addition to banknotes and cash (including a crown piece) which have now taken the place of all other forms of gift, the pensioners receive some of the world's most interesting coins presented in a small leather purse, with as many pence as the monarch has years of age. The recipients themselves number as many men and as many women as the monarch has years. In the days before base metal money, the amount was made up from silver pennies, twopences, threepences and fourpences and are still, today, struck in silver and polished like proof coins.

IN THE NEWS

WEEK 1   **"Thousands Strike Over Pay and Prices"** About 1.6 million workers joined the TUC's call for a one-day strike, in protest at the government's pay restraint policy and price rises.

"Hush Hush Nixon" President Nixon stepped into the Watergate bugging scandal by banning all White house staff from divulging whether they had discussed the affair with him.

WEEK 2   **"Population Day"** Britain's first mobile birth control-vasectomy centre at Waterloo Station, London, opened to the public for advice and consultation.

WEEK 3   **"Nixon Did Know"** A star public witness said Mr Nixon had been involved in offers of clemency to those on trial for the Watergate bugging if they would agree to go to jail for a year and keep silent.

"Royal Navy to Protect Trawlers" Britain sends Royal Navy ships to protect trawlers in the disputed Icelandic 50-mile zone as the 'cod wars' escalate.

WEEK 4   **"Astronauts Fail to Repair Skylab"** Three American astronauts rendezvoused with the crippled Skylab space station launched on May 14. They failed to repair the damage and failed to dock at least three times because the latches would not fasten on.

"Princess Anne is to Marry Lieutenant Mark Phillips" The couple became engaged at Easter and will marry in November.

HERE IN BRITAIN

"The 'Little Man' Snubs Rolls"

The great British Rolls-Royce Motors share offer has been given the brush-off by small investors when, salvaged from the bankrupt parent group, it offered over £38m worth of stocks and shares to the public. Only £8m was applied for from individuals leaving the city to pick up the rest.

One stockbroker said, *"It's a floparoo and a blow to our national pride. When Mothercare went public last June, the issue pulled in £142m. Rolls-Royce is pathetic compared to that."* Labour minister Anthony Wedgewood Benn was blamed, the previous week he said a future Labour government might nationalise the company without compensation.

AROUND THE WORLD

"Matchless in Mozambique"

"Excuse me senhor, but have you a match?" The smoker's earnest request is a common one at the pavement cafes in Lourenço Marques. Along the tree-lined avenues, African urchins clutching enamel bowls full of cashew nuts attempt to sell them by the bag to the mainly white cafe customers, jostling with shoeshine boys and cripples selling lottery tickets.

It is matches which are most in demand, however. They are among scores of imported items, ranging from luxury toilet soap to cars, which have become scarce because of the island's enforced economic independence from Portugal.

In The News

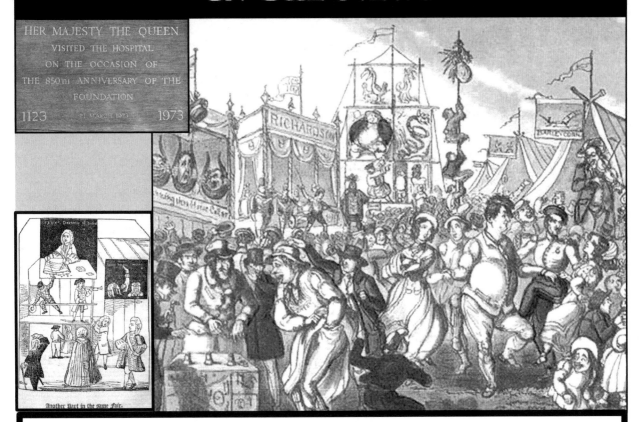

HER MAJESTY THE QUEEN
VISITED THE HOSPITAL
ON THE OCCASION OF
THE 850th ANNIVERSARY OF THE
FOUNDATION
1123   21 MARCH 1973   1973

Another Bart in the same Fair.

ST BARTS IS 850 YEARS' OLD

To celebrate the 850th anniversary of the foundation of St Bartholomew's Hospital, London's ancient and disreputable fair is being revived for one day only. Originally a major trading event for cloth as well as a pleasure fair, the event drew crowds from all classes of English society and featured puppet-shows, wrestlers, fire-eaters, dwarfs, dancing bears, performing monkeys and caged tigers, all vying for attention with contortionists and tight-rope walkers. Astrologers cast horoscopes and miraculous medicines were hawked. Food and beer vendors bellowed for custom and there were plentiful supplies of toys, gingerbread, mousetraps, puppies, purses and singing birds in a general bedlam of shouts, fiddles, drums and rattles. The fair was a great opportunity for pickpockets and also for prostitutes. The fair was closed down by prudish Victorians in 1855, for 'encouraging debauchery and public disorder'.

It was customary for the Lord Mayor of London to open the fair and the present-day Lord Mayor performed the honours for this year's celebrations, organised by a consultant anaesthetist at Bart's and his colleagues, who took great pains to revive such old attractions as were practical and legal. In addition, there was a balloon race fuelled by the hospital's anaesthetic department and a performance of 'William Harvey's Revolutionary Circus', a musical play specially written for the occasion, concerned with Harvey's discovery of the circulation of the blood which included 'a light-hearted song and dance routine weaving in and out of a 12-foot-high model of a heart'.

This modern celebration lacked one essential element though, from 'The Postman' of 1701, *"The Tiger in Bartholomew Fair, that yesterday gave such satisfaction to persons of all qualities by pulling the feathers so nicely from live fowls, will, at the request of several persons, do the same this day"*.

IN THE NEWS

WEEK 1   **"Greece Abolishes Monarchy"** The Greek regime, established by military coup in 1967, became a republic following a second coup, led by Mr George Papadopoulos.

"Russian Rival to Concorde Crashes" The Tupolev 144 disintegrated after a mid-air explosion over the Paris Air Show and crashed on to a town.

WEEK 2   **"Equal Pay: What Are You Doing About It?"** The Government warned firms not to wait to implement the Equal Pay Act 1970, which makes it unlawful to discriminate between men and women after the end of 1975.

WEEK 3   **"Midget Sub Rescue"** Trapped off the Florida coast for over 24 hours after they became entangled in wreckage, two crew of the research submarine 'Sea Link' were brought up alive, but two others perished.

"Royal Yacht Recruiting" For the first time, the Ministry of Defence has been forced to send out an SOS for crew for the yacht. Hitherto there has always been a waiting list.

WEEK 4   **"Senator Stabbed 50 Times"** The murder of Belfast's best known Catholic opposition politicians, Senator Paddy Wilson, marks a new and sinister phase in Northern Ireland.

"Top Players Boycott Wimbledon" Several of the world's top seeds did not play on the instructions of their union ATP, in support of the Yugoslav player Nikola Pilić who was suspended in May.

HERE IN BRITAIN

"Genteel Protestors"

Villagers from Ditchling in Sussex do not want the juggernauts thundering through their village taking shortcuts to Brighton and Newhaven. The organisers were at pains to hold a 'respectable' protest. Villagers held placards inscribed 'They shall not pass' and 'Save our village' and marched to and fro across the narrow crossroads causing long traffic jams.

The scouts were on parade in uniform and respectable ladies with blue rinses distributed leaflets and gossiped about their gardens while retired gentlemen in club ties led the village children in chanting slogans. Miss Vera Lynn, not until now the most militant of show business personalities, held a banner.

AROUND THE WORLD

"Skylab Splash Down"

Three American astronauts splashed down safely in the Pacific after a record breaking 28 days in space. They left behind, the Skylab space laboratory, which had so many difficulties since it was launched in May, and even another last-minute hitch resulted in a 10-minute delay before the astronauts undocked their Apollo spacecraft and headed for Earth.

The main question now is how the three men have been affected by the long period of weightlessness inside Skylab. They appear to have adapted well and as they hurtled down towards the Pacific, Captain Charles Conrad said, *"We're all in good shape. Everything's OK."*

A Camera Inside A Cigarette Packet

A Transmitter Inside Fake Dog Poo

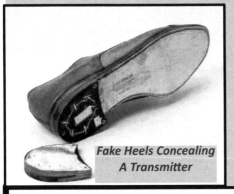

Fake Heels Concealing A Transmitter

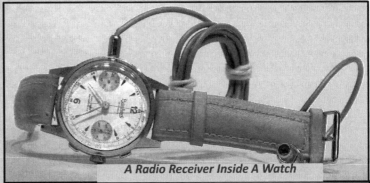

A Radio Receiver Inside A Watch

SOMEONE, SOMEWHERE COULD BE LISTENING

In the aftermath of the Watergate and the Lambton scandal, the lack of control over the manufacture, sale and use of secret bugging devices in Britain is causing widespread concern in political and legal circles. An extensive range of advanced surveillance equipment is being made in this country and turnover of the industry is estimated at well over £1m a year.

Advertised in their brochures are, undetectable telephone tapping equipment, 'bugs' concealed in harmless looking pens, ashtrays and cigarette lighters (£25), custom built briefcases (£140) containing concealed devices and microphones designed to eavesdrop from the vibrations on walls, windows and doors. This month an attempt has been made to introduce a highly sophisticated new electronic spying device to the British market. Already in wide-spread use in America, where it is known as the 'infinity bug', this £232 device would enable a private telephone set to be turned into an eavesdropping transmitter with a world range. With the Monitel Mark II connected to a telephone line, it is possible to monitor the activities in a room from any point in the world having direct dialling to that telephone line. The unit is small, easy to conceal and requires no power supply. There is nothing illegal about manufacturing or advertising bugging devices in Britain although there are laws that make it illegal to operate them.

This month also, the Post Office is testing a new type of security apparatus which allows telephone calls, telex messages and computer data to be transmitted over private or public networks without fear of electronic bugging. Made by Datotek, which started business by developing electronic systems of cryptography for American oil companies, including encoding telex messages. The security methods used for this purpose have been extended to telephone conversations and computer data.

JULY 1973

IN THE NEWS

WEEK 1   **"Canadian Tour"** The Queen and the Duke of Edinburgh have arrived in Prince Edward Island, the smallest of Canada's provinces, to celebrate the centenary of the Island's decision to join the confederation.

"Riots at Longkesh" Fierce riots in the Long Kesh prison left 21 inmates, eight soldiers and four warders with minor injuries. All the prisoners were convicted republicans holding 'political' status.

WEEK 2   **"Paul Getty's Grandson Kidnapped"** Paul Getty III, teenage grandson of the oil millionaire, one of the richest men in the world, was kidnapped in Italy.

"Bahamas' Independence Day" Prince Charles hosted a reception at Government House, Nassau, for dignitaries from 52 countries after over 300 years of British sovereignty.

WEEK 3   **"Tape Records of Police Questioning"** Magistrates are calling for experiments to be carried out using tape recorders during police interrogation of suspects.

WEEK 4   **"Final Deal for Thalidomide Victims"** After an 11-year legal battle, the Distillers Company who marketed thalidomide have agreed to pay more than £20 million in compensation to those born with birth defects.

"Chaotic Meeting of Belfast Assembly" The Northern Ireland Assembly met for the first time in Stormont, Belfast, but the two-hour debate was disrupted by a group of hard-line loyalists led by Reverend Ian Paisley.

HERE IN BRITAIN
"Mr Spassky Has Hollywood Treatment"

With chess now firmly established as a branch of show business, the start of the week-long European team championships in Bath was attended by a large crowd of devotees and world press. With an almost impassive face, Mr Boris Spassky, who leads the Russian team and is now well used to the Hollywood treatment of chess, eased through the ring of lenses and lights, shook hands with his opponent and smoked a cigarette elegantly as cameramen crouched and clicked.

Thirty-two chess boards, with attendant clocks, free cigarettes and matches, were laid out on eight green tables, waiting for the start.

AROUND THE WORLD
"France Fixes Limit"

The two million Parisians who left the capital on the first of the two great holiday exoduses of the year, and the several million provincials and foreigners driving through France, will have to keep a close watch on their speedometers. For the first time, in spite of a barrage of protests, the Government has plucked up its courage and imposed a basic speed limit of 60 miles an hour on all roads except motorways.

The question is, how to enforce these regulations? It has been estimated it would need about 18,000 additional police and gendarmerie to ensure that the new speed limit is observed.

TAKE AN EU LETTER MISS JONES

Hundreds of secretaries queued up to be interviewed for 150 jobs with the European Parliament this month. The Parliament had advertised for British secretaries earlier this year in restrained, bureaucratic terminology, without catching the eye of enough applicants of high quality. Its latest advertisement was more irresistibly conspicuous. It invited anybody interested in earning £4,000 a year, with 30 working days' holiday plus public holidays, her own apartment, two free flights home and the glamour of foreign travel - to Luxembourg- to 'drop in' at a London hotel for interview. So many turned up that the queue stretched out of the door and out of sight down the side of the hotel, some girls having travelled overnight from all over Britain.

Head of recruitment for the European Parliament estimated that 500 girls had turned up for the morning session and more dropped in continually for three more sessions throughout the day. *"The girls will have to work a 40-hour week"*, she said, *"we are not offering them free Continental holidays. For that money they will have to work very hard and do a great deal of overtime."*

Many dropped out when they learnt that speaking a second European language was a necessary qualification, the advert had merely stated in modest print that it was a desirable asset. Those who stayed were interviewed and then put through fiendishly demanding tests. They had to copy-type a page of poorly handwritten European jargon in the second language of their choice, then speed-type English at 50 words a minute and take shorthand at 120 words a minute on the indecipherable subject of the floating pound.

Said one, *"The advertisement was rather overenthusiastic, in fact, a bit of a come-on, but it shows the demand in the secretarial market. Anyone can learn to type, and at that price, everyone is going to."*

AUGUST 1973

IN THE NEWS

WEEK 1

"Dozens Die in Resort Fire" More than 30 people died in a fire which gutted Summerland a £2m leisure resort in the Isle of Man. Police investigations concluded the fire was deliberate.

"Taylor and Burton to Divorce" Liz Taylor is ending her fifth marriage and Richard Burton his second, nine years after they married in Montreal.

WEEK 2

"Skylab Spider Web Success" Arabella, a spider on board Skylab 2 was disoriented by weightlessness at first but now, on day 13, has produced a web *"like one you would find on the ground"*.

"Butlins Fire Increases Fears" A new controversy has broken out over holiday camp safety following a £1m fire at Butlins largest camp, Pwllheli in North Wales. No-one was hurt.

WEEK 3

"Bomb in Hampstead Shopping Centre" Security clampdown by Scotland Yard after a bomb wrecked the front of a carpet store in Hampstead. No one was injured.

"Spate of IRA Fire and Letter Bombs" Six letter bombs, built into paperbacks on a musical theme, were sent to London addresses and nine fire-bombs found at West End stores.

WEEK 4

"Stock Exchange, Baker Street and No 10 Bombs" Two people were hurt at the Stock Exchange; the bomb was defused at Baker Street and a letter bomb was disarmed at Number 10.

HERE IN BRITAIN

"A Smooth and Silent Ride"

It used to be said that the loudest noise in a Rolls-Royce travelling at a hundred miles an hour was the tick of the clock. In British Rail's new high-speed train, it was the discreet clatter of coffee cups and a subdued rumble from beneath – and this was at 135mph.

Britain's new high-speed train made a demonstration run from London to Darlington, ahead of its passenger trials later this month and service on various routes in 1975. Journey times on the long inter-city routes will all be cut and save up to an hour on the London to Edinburgh route.

AROUND THE WORLD

"Basketball Battle"

American and Cuban athletes fought a bloody, five-minute battle in Moscow before several hundred stunned Russian spectators at a World University Games basketball match. The Cubans swung wooden folding chairs at the Americans, who fought back with their fists. One American was knocked unconscious and blood and broken glass littered the floor when officials finally brought the situation under control.

The fight broke out 90 seconds before the end of the game, which the Americans won by 98 to 70, when a Cuban player kicked an American player and brought him down. The Russian crowd's cheers for the Cubans changed to boos, jeers and whistles.

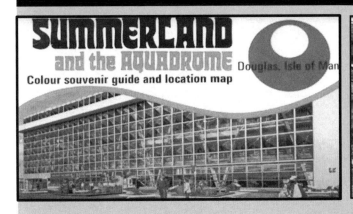

Before the fire

The fire rages

After the fire

SUMMERLAND, LEISURE FOR THE FUTURE

The Isle of Man has been a popular holiday spot since Edwardian times with 227 square miles of countryside and hundred miles of coastline and a choice of eight resort centres. It is the place for a family holiday, but the summer weather is cool and wet. Town councillors decided that as tourism accounted for half the island's income, something was needed to provide sufficient wet weather amenities. 'Summerland' was the answer. It was the biggest and most expensive project ever undertaken by the island of 56,000 people. It cost £2m, covered 31 acres of floor space on the north end of Douglas seafront and, with several storeys, rose to 100ft.

Summerland opened in July 1971 and *'was the largest entertainments complex under one roof in the world. A futuristic leisure life, one for the twenty-first century even, with paving stones heated from underneath. Yet this is here and now, a scientific and engineering marvel that makes it one of the latest wonders of the world. Cocooned in a protective sheath of transparent acrylic sheeting is the equivalent of a holiday village where up to 10,000 people at any one time can wander at will."* Summerland contained restaurants, bars, amusement arcades, staged a funfair, a discotheque, colour television lounge and a sundeck. One of its main features was the Sundome, where tourists could laze under a battery of ultra- violet and infrared lights to acquire an instant suntan. Alongside, in the Aquadrome, there were two heated swimming pools, and a complex of sauna, Turkish and vapour baths.

Visitors numbers grew by 7.6% but the disaster struck on the 2nd of August 1973 when a fire spread through the complex killing 50 people and severely injuring 80, and it now lies in smouldering ruins.

IN THE NEWS

WEEK 1   **"Midget Sub Men Rescued"** Two men who had been submerged off the Irish coast whilst laying telecommunication cables, were brought safely to the surface.

WEEK 2   **"Bomb Blasts Rock Central London"** Two IRA bombs brought chaos to central London. The first was at King's Cross Station and the second at a snack bar at Euston station.

"Channel Tunnel to Go Ahead" The Government said 'yes' to the Anglo-French project but said the opening of the new, third, London airport at Maplin, Essex, would be put back until 1982.

WEEK 3   **"Blaze from Boys' Cigarette"** A cigarette, shared by three Liverpool schoolboys, was not stubbed out properly and caused the fire at Summerland last month in which 49 people died.

"Explosion at Chelsea Army Barracks" Five people including two soldiers were injured when a bomb exploded at the Duke of York's barracks, home to the Parachute Regiment.

WEEK 4   **"Concorde Slashes Atlantic Flight Time"** Concorde has made its first non-stop crossing of the Atlantic in record-breaking time. Washington to Paris in 3hrs 32 minutes.

"Ford Strike Settled" After two weeks, the loss of 7,000 cars and a cost of £7m, a man sacked for attacking his foreman was reinstated and workers returned.

HERE IN BRITAIN
"Bin the Bomb"

Eight children found a bomb on an office doorstep in Five Ways, Birmingham, and accidentally defused it. The children were walking home after playing in a local 'den', saw the plastic sandwich box in the office doorway and investigated.

They thought at first the 'reel' inside was fishing tackle but then realised it was an alarm clock and after pulling the wires out – which luckily made it safe – realised it was a bomb and ran fifty yards to put it in the grit bin. They telephoned the police but *"they seemed a long time coming so two of us ran to a local police station."*

AROUND THE WORLD
"Male Chauvinism Vanquished"

Mrs Billy Jean King, the Wimbledon champion, soundly defeated Mr Bobby Riggs, a self-proclaimed 'male chauvinist'. 30,472 people had crowded into Houston's Astrodome for the match where Mrs King arrived in a gold-coloured litter, borne by athletes from a neighbouring university.

Her opponent made an equally flamboyant entry in a rickshaw, pulled by six professional models. Before play started, Mr Riggs presented Mrs King with a six- foot-long lollipop, saying that she was going to be 'a sucker for my lobs'. Mrs King responded by handing him a small, live pig - a hint that he was a 'male chauvinist pig'.

IN THE NEWS

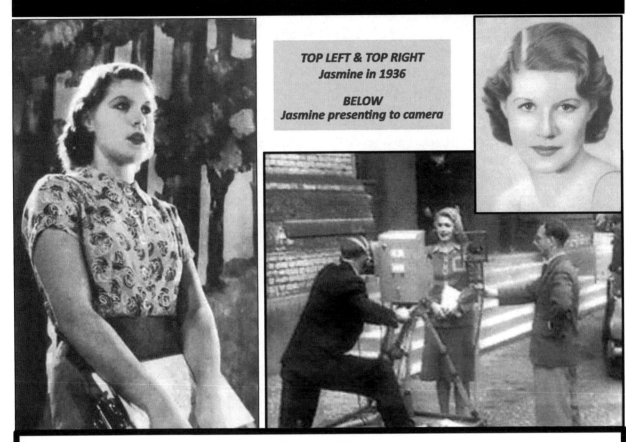

TOP LEFT & TOP RIGHT
Jasmine in 1936

BELOW
Jasmine presenting to camera

MISS BLIGH RETURNS

Miss Jasmine Bligh, one of the first two women television announcers is being brought back to the television screen. Miss Bligh, who announced the original programmes of the BBC from Alexandra Palace in 1936, will present a fortnightly programme on Fridays dealing with people's emotional and physical problems on Thames Television's daily magazine 'Good Afternoon'.

In 1936, with the beginning of television transmissions, the BBC relaxed its proscription of female announcers and advertised the job. There were 1,100 applicants from whom Jasmine Bligh and Elizabeth Cowell were selected to announce beside Leslie Mitchell. She was hired at £350 a year and worked from 11 am to 11 pm five days in one week and two days in the next. In those pioneering days women announcers were issued with two evening dresses and two skirts and blouses to wear. There were no teleprompting devices and no auto-cues, they simply stood in front of the camera and spoke lines they had learnt by heart. Miss Bligh, now 60, said yesterday, "*It was a continuous, glorious laugh. There were only about 300 people altogether working in television, so everyone knew everyone else.*"

After a year she became bored with announcing and as a side-line, became the 'Pearl White' of the television screen, performing such stunts as trick motorcycling, being rescued by firemen and playing tennis on the Centre Court at Wimbledon wearing a boater. Television ended with the war, but Miss Bligh returned to make the opening announcement when it started again afterwards. After a year she retired, married and now lives near Newbury, where she runs and drives the only known mobile second-hand clothes shop in the world. Announcing her return, Miss Bligh said, "*I am apprehensive, but naturally delighted at the way things have come full circle.*"

IN THE NEWS

WEEK 1   **"Elsie Tanner Leaves The Street"** Pat Phoenix suddenly departed Coronation Street, saying she was bored to tears with the role and was returning to the stage where her real ambitions had always been.

"Arab States Attack Israeli Forces" Egyptian armoured forces break through the Israeli line on the eastern bank of the Suez Canal and along the Golan Heights seized by Israel from Syria in 1967.

WEEK 2   **"Spiro Agnew Quits"** America's Vice President resigned after pleading guilty to income-tax fraud. It is thought other charges of bribery and corruption will be dropped.

"Commercial Radio Joins UK Airwaves" LBC (London Broadcasting Company), Britain's first independent radio station, began broadcasting.

WEEK 3   **"£1m Damage to Brighton Pier"** The Palace Pier was severely damaged by a 70-ton barge which broke loose from its moorings at the end of the pier during a gale.

"Dalai Lama makes first UK visit The spiritual leader of Tibetan Buddhists, the Dalai Lama, arrived in Britain for a 10-day tour. It is the first time he has been to the UK.

WEEK 4   **"No Landing for the Osmonds"** Manchester airport barred the American pop group the Osmond Brothers from flying into the city for a concert, 24 hours after 20 children were hurt when a balcony gave way at Heathrow.

HERE IN BRITAIN

""Soldier Bakes Princess Anne's Cake"

In a locked room in Aldershot, the home of the British Army, Princess Anne's wedding cake was maturing and waiting for its coat of icing, shrouded by the sort of secrecy usually reserved for a new nuclear weapon. The bride's mother will not have to pay the £25 the cake has cost to make as it will be the gift from the Army Catering Corps officers.

Only two men have been allowed into the 'cake room', somewhere in the corps' 12-storey training centre, a senior officer and the unnamed baker. It has taken six weeks from the mixing to the completion of the masterpiece.

AROUND THE WORLD

""Queen Opens Sydney Opera House"

The Queen opened the Sydney Opera House this month, launching a giant 'ship of sail' amid a great spectacle of carnival and colour. More than one million spectators crammed the foreshores of Sydney harbour for the day-long festivities.

It was 14 years seven months and 18 days since the work began on the opera house. The Queen recalled that the construction has not been without controversy and said, "Extreme controversy attended the building of the pyramids, yet they stand today 4,000 years later, acknowledged as one of the wonders of the world. I believe this will be so for the Sydney Opera House."

THE NEWLY REOPENED CARNABY STREET

CARNABY STREET RESTYLED

Carnaby Street, the epitome of Swinging London, was officially reopened this month, having been refurbished to suit its trendy international image. The street and its adjacent courts and alleys are now closed to traffic between 11 am and 8 pm and this pedestrian precinct has been paved overall in gaudy geometric patterns with orange, white, yellow and black nylon tiles. They are slightly elastic, so pedestrians feel like pawns on a vast, spongy chess board. Twenty streetlamps from Munich look like giant egg timers, double spheres balanced on silver columns 14ft high, and other new street furniture include 7' 6" high poster drums, trees in tubs, benches and litter bins. Huge, illuminated signs hang above the street to flash 'Carnaby Street Welcomes the World'. The crowded little shops selling unisex clothes, gangster trousers, 'Hello Sailor' T-shirts and *'the largest collection of old clothes in the world'*, hung out banners to celebrate the reopening.

At Inderwick's, 'England's oldest pipe makers', the owner, surrounded by briars, meerschaums and calabashes, said, *"Of course, we were here before Carnaby Street began to swing. I think that the pattern of the street paving is hideous, and I do not see why they had to import lamp posts from Germany. But it is a better place for shopping without cars."* The girl selling culottes made of chain mail and other startling gear in 'Sweet Fanny Adams' said, *"Now that the holiday peak is over business has fallen off, but the redecoration has made it a much gayer place to work and shop in."* The street took its name from a house built there in the seventeenth century. It first became a street market, then a row of Victorian shops selling seedy clothing and in the early 1960s, *'the fashion flair of Carnaby Street became the trend-setter for young people on every continent'.*

NOVEMBER 1973

IN THE NEWS

WEEK 1 **"Helicopter Jail-Break"** Three Provisional IRA leaders were snatched in a hijacked helicopter from the exercise yard of Mountjoy prison, Dublin.

"Oil: Arabs Turn the Screw" The Arab nations cut oil production to the West by a further 5% bringing the total cut to 25% since the start of the Arab Israeli war.

WEEK 2 **"Paul Getty III Ear in Post"** An envelope containing his severed right ear was delivered to the offices of a Rome newspaper. The 17-year-old grandson of millionaire Paul Getty has been missing since July 10.

"State of Emergency" Overtime bans by miners and electricity worker have caused shortages. Overseas trade figures are the worst in history and Bank lending rates have been raised to 13%.

WEEK 3 **"IRA Eight on Hunger Strike"** The protest began immediately after they received life sentences at Winchester Crown Court for planting the car bombs that exploded in London on March 8.

WEEK 4 **"Army Deposes 'Hated' Greek President"** The Greek Government, and self-appointed President George Papadopoulos, have been toppled by the country's armed forces after weeks of unrest.

"Petrol Coupons Ready" But Saudi Arabia has promised to supply Britain – 'a friendly country' with the same level of oil as in the 9 months leading up to last September.

HERE IN BRITAIN

"Herbs, Spurs and Greyhounds"

The Duke of Cornwall, also known as the Prince of Wales, visited the Duchy of Cornwall to receive for the first time his feudal 'dues'. A load of firewood, a grey cloak, 100 old shillings, a pound of pepper, a hunting bow, gilt spurs, a pound of herbs, a Neptune sized salmon spear, a pair of gloves like Hell's Angel gauntlets, and two greyhounds.

The 'dues' were first paid by duchy tenants to the Black Prince, the first Duke of Cornwall, when he rode down for hunting but for many years the duchy has also collected substantial rents from the tenants.

AROUND THE WORLD

"Mrs Beeton Could Save Your Life"

In Paris a man was sent to prison for eight years for killing his second wife - as he did his first - because her cooking was not up to cordon bleu standard. Seventeen years ago, enraged with her *undercooked* meat, he threw his first wife out of bed so violently that she broke her neck.

After seven years in prison, he was released and married again. Then one Sunday he quarrelled with this wife over an *overcooked* roast. The jury found that he did not intend to murder his wife and the judge agreed that *'good cooking is an important part of married life'.*

In The News

The Royal Wedding

On 11th November, Princess Anne married Captain Mark Phillips in what was only the tenth, truly Royal Wedding, to be held in Westminster Abbey. History records several royal marriages 'at Westminster' but that does not necessarily mean Westminster Abbey and might have referred to St Stephen's Chapel in the Palace of Westminster.

The first recorded royal wedding in the abbey was that of King Henry I when he married Matilda, the daughter of Malcolm Canmore, King of Scotland. Matilda had been brought up in the convent at Romsey, Hampshire, and there were scandalous rumours that she was a nun and therefore unmarriageable even to the King. However, the Archbishop of Canterbury pronounced that she was not a nun, and, according to the Anglo-Saxon Chronicle, the English were delighted to see a Norman king take a wife of *'England's right kingly kin'*.

In 1269 Prince Edmund 'Crouchback', Earl of Lancaster, the younger son of Henry III, married Aveline, daughter of William de Forz, Count of Albermarle in the abbey and then there was a gap of more than six centuries until the next royal wedding in the abbey. The three latest royal weddings were those of the Queen and the Duke of Edinburgh in 1947, Princess Margaret and Lord Snowdon in 1960, and Princess Alexandria and Mr Angus Ogilvy in 1963.

Princess Anne wore an embroidered Tudor-style wedding dress with a high collar and medieval sleeves and Lieutenant Phillips was in the full scarlet and blue uniform of his regiment, the Queen's Dragoon Guards. It is only the second time in more than 200 years that a member of the British royal family has married a commoner. The previous commoner to marry into the royal family was the Queen Mother in 1923.

DECEMBER 1973

IN THE NEWS

WEEK 1 **"No Petrol Rationing Yet"** But a mandatory maximum speed limit of 50mph on all roads brought in to conserve fuel and an appeal for workers to 'car share' and offer lifts.

"Israel's Founding Father Dies" David Ben-Gurion, a founder of the Israeli state and its first prime minister, died aged 87. Mr Ben-Gurion died from a brain haemorrhage he suffered two weeks ago.

WEEK 2 **"Britain at Bay"** Miners' overtime ban causes power cuts: Go slow by rail drivers cripples services; Oil crisis which Arab countries warn will get worse; Pressure on the £ and Heath's 'Stage Three' pay-and-prices policy under threat.

"Sunningdale Agreement Signed" Tripartite talks on Northern Ireland held at Sunningdale, Berkshire, ended in the signing of an historic agreement to set up a Council of Ireland.

WEEK 3 **"Paul Getty III Released"** The 17-year-old grandson of the American millionaire, was found cold and exhausted at a roadside in Italy. The ransom of £1.2m had been paid.

"Sixty People Injured in London" Two car bombs exploded outside a Home Office building in Westminster and near Pentonville prison, and two parcel bombs, at a temporary sorting office in Westminster and a shopping arcade in Hampstead.

WEEK 4 **"Spanish Prime Minister Assassinated"** The Spanish Prime Minister, Admiral Luis Carrero Blanco, was killed in a car bomb attack in Madrid.

HERE IN BRITAIN

"5,000 Calls a Day"

70 civil servants at the Department of Trade and Industry, manning telephones 24 hours a day, bore the brunt of the confusion and uncertainty over the Government's energy-saving measures and the 'three-day-week' to start on the 31st.

Whilst most calls were serious, others included: *"Can I still use oil in an Aladdin's lamp during a pantomime"* and *"Can I install fairy lights for the church crib".* On the highly complex calls people were advised, *"Our whole purpose is to cut the consumption of energy. Try to do without as much power as possible, even it means taking out half the light bulbs."*

AROUND THE WORLD

"Lottery Instant Millionaires"

Spain's huge Christmas lottery, known as El Gordo, "the fat one", gave away £63m. There were nearly 200,000 cash prizes, all of them tax-free, with 18 of more than £500,000 each. The cost of a whole ticket is 10,000 pesetas (£77), but most Spaniards buy a decimo, or a one-tenth share of the number, or even smaller shares.

Every family in Spain has several small 'participations' in tickets held by others. Shopkeepers distribute vouchers worth a tiny percentage as Christmas gifts for their customers. Office workers pool their money to buy tickets and each of them holds a fraction of one or more numbers.

CHRISTMAS HOLIDAY FOR PIT PONIES

In a month of unremitting misery, this Christmas, horses were at the centre of the only pleasant aspect of the coal crisis. Because of the overtime ban, the pit ponies who live underground were brought to the surface for an unexpected winter holiday. Usually, they come up for their three weeks' annual holiday only in the summer. The ponies of Lady Windsor Colliery in the Rhondda were installed in temporary stables in the colliery stores from where the manager took them for walks and gave them oats during the Christmas break.

A pit pony stands 13 to 15 hands, has the build of a miniature carthorse, and enjoys the official title of colliery horse. Even in highly mechanized pits the colliery horse has an important role and whilst no horse pulls coal today, they do the jobs that machines cannot do and go where it would be too expensive to take machines. *"He is self-propelled, simple to manage, turns in his own length, and with regular, love and care hardly ever breaks down or needs an overhaul."* 25 years ago there were about 5,000 pit horses in Wales but now there are only 85, working a 48-hour week in 20 collieries. They are geldings chosen for steady temperament, live in well-lit, well-ventilated stables, are free from disease and are certainly not blind.

The bond between miners and the animals they work with is renowned in the coalfields and stories of the faithfulness and cussedness of the horses are legion. Horses have saved lives by halting in their tracks and refusing to budge seconds before a roof fall and miners with broken lamps have been led to safety through pitch black tunnels by hanging on to them. It is said that a horse once pressed its body against a collapsing wall while men escaped.

1970 - 1974

1970:

Jan: The age of majority for most legal purposes was reduced from 21 to 18 under terms of the Family Law Reform Act 1969.

Mar: Ian Smith declares Rhodesia a Republic and the British government refuses to recognise the new state.

1971:

Feb: Decimal Day. The UK and the Republic of Ireland both change to decimal currency.

Mar: The 'Daily Sketch', Britain's oldest tabloid newspaper is absorbed by the 'Daily Mail' after 62 years.

1972:

June: The 'Watergate' scandal begins in Richard Nixon's administration in the US.

Sep: The school leaving age in the UK was raised from 15 to 16 for pupils leaving at the end of the academic year.

1973:

Jan: The United Kingdom joins the European Economic Community, later to become the EU.

Sep: The IRA detonate bombs in Manchester and Victoria Station London and two days later, Oxford St. and Sloane Square.

1974:

Jan: Until March, the 3-day week is introduced by the Conservative Government to conserve electricity during the miners' strike.

Nov: 21 people are killed and 182 injured when the IRA set bombs in two Birmingham pubs.

1974: McDonald's open their first UK restaurant in South London. The traditional café was losing out, slow ordering and service with food served at tables was not as appealing as the clean, fast service and lower prices of this new fast food.

1974: In February, Harold Wilson becomes Prime Minister for the second time (first 1964-70) with a minority Government after Edward Heath resigns having failed to clinch a coalition with the Liberals. In the second general election of the year in October, Labour win with a majority of only 3 seats.

In June and July 1976, the UK experienced a heat wave. Temperatures peak at 35.9° and the whole country suffers a severe drought. Forest fires broke out, crops failed, and reservoirs dried up causing serious water shortages. The heatwave also produced swarms of ladybirds across the south and east.

On the 7th June,1977, more than one million people lined the streets of London to watch the Queen and Prince Phillip lead a procession in the golden state coach, to St Paul's at the start of a week of the Queen's Silver Jubilee celebrations – 25 years on the throne. People all over the country held street or village parties to celebrate, more than 100,000 cards were received by the Queen and 30,000 Jubilee medals were given out.

1975 - 1979

1975:
Feb: Margaret Thatcher defeats Edward Heath to become the first female leader of the Conservative Party.

Apr: The Vietnam War ends with the Fall of Saigon to the Communists. South Vietnam surrenders unconditionally.

1976:
Mar: Harold Wilson announces his resignation as Prime Minister and James Callaghan is elected to the position in April.

Oct: The Intercity 125 high speed passenger train is introduced. Initially Paddington to Bristol and south Wales.

1977:
Jan: Jimmy Carter is sworn in as the 39th President of the United States, succeeding Gerald Ford.

Sep: Freddie Laker launches his 'Skytrain' with a single fare, Gatwick to New York, at £59 compared to £189.

1978:
Aug: Louise Brown becomes the world's first human born 'in vitro fertilisation' – test tube baby.

Nov: An industrial dispute shuts down The Times newspaper – until November 1979.

1979:
Mar: Airey Neave, politician and WW2 veteran, is blown up in the House of Commons car park by the Irish National Liberation Army.

May: Margaret Thatcher becomes the first female Prime Minister of the United Kingdom. The Conservatives win a 43 seat majority.

THE HOME

Increasing Comfort and Prosperity

Homes became brighter and more comfortable in the 1970's. Teenagers could lie on the 'impossible to clean', loopy shag pile carpet watching films on VHS video cassettes or watch live programmes on the family's colour television set.

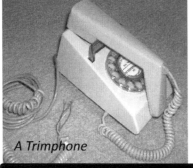

A Trimphone

The ubiquitous macramé owl, or plant holder complete with trailing spider plant, might dangle in the corner adjacent to the bulky, stone faced, rustic fireplace. Bathroom suites were often Avocado green and 'downstairs loos' were a statement of the houseowners ideals! If you were one of the 35% of households in Britain to own a telephone, you could catch up with friends and family on the new 'warbling' Trimphone, maybe sitting on your bright, floral covered couch.

Labour Saving Devices

The previous decade had been prosperous and the advances in technology continued such that by the 1970s, most households had many labour-saving devices. Sales of freezers rose rapidly in the 70s and by 1974, one in ten households had a freezer - mainly full of peas, chips and fish fingers but also ice cream, previously a rare treat, and in large quantities. Bulk buying food meant less time shopping and the Magimix food processor which added a choice of blades and attachments to a standard liquidiser, made home cooking more adventurous.

Teenage Home Entertainment

Teenagers covered their bedroom walls with posters of their favourite bands and actors, ranging from Rod Stewart and the Boomtown Rats to Olivia Newton-John and Robert Redford. The lucky ones listening to top ten singles on their own stereo record deck which had replaced the old Dansette player.

If they wanted to play the new video games, they typically went to an arcade, but in 1975, Atari PONG was released, the first commercially successful video game you could play at home on your television. Based on a simple two-dimensional graphical representation of a tennis-like game, two players used paddles to hit a ball back and forth on a black and white screen. It captivated audiences and its success influenced developers to invent more and increasingly sophisticated games for the home market.

The luxury of a Goblin Teasmade, the automatic tea-maker and alarm clock, revolutionised early morning tea.

ART AND CULTURE

1970 - 1974

1970 Laurence Olivier becomes the first actor to be made a Lord. He is given a life peerage in the Queen's Birthday Honours list.
The first Glastonbury Festival was held, called the Worthy Farm Pop Festival. About 1500 attended.

1971 Coco Chanel, the French fashion designer died. (Born 1883)
The 'Blue Peter' presenters buried a time capsule in the grounds of BBC Television Centre, due to be opened on the first episode in 2000.
Mr Tickle, the first of the Mr Men books is published.

1972 'Jesus Christ Superstar', the Tim Rice & Andrew Lloyd Webber musical opens in the West End.
John Betjeman is appointed Poet Laureate.

1973 The British Library is established by merger of the British Museum Library & the National Lending Library for Science & Technology.
Series 1 of the BBC sitcom, 'Last of the Summer Wine' begins. There are eventually, 31 series.

1974 'Tinker, Tailor, Soldier, Spy' the first of John Le Carré's novel featuring the ageing spymaster, George Smiley, is published.
The Terracotta Army of Qin Shi Huang, thousands of life-size clay models of soldiers, horses and chariots, is discovered at Xi'an in China.

Milton Keynes Shopping Centre

1975 - 1979

1975 Donald Coggan is enthroned as the Archbishop of Canterbury.
Bill Gates and Paul Allen found Microsoft in Albuquerque, New Mexico.

1976 Trevor Nunn's memorable production of 'Macbeth' opens at Stratford-upon-Avon, with Ian McKellan and Judi Dench in the lead roles.
The Royal National Theatre on the South Bank opens.
Agatha Christie's last novel, Sleeping Murder, a Miss Marple story is published posthumously.

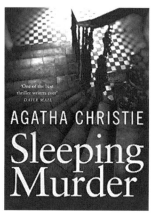

1977 Luciano Pavarotti makes his television debut singing in Puccini's La Boheme in the television debut of 'Live from the Met'.
Mike Leigh's satire on the aspirations and tastes of the new middle class emerging in the 70's, 'Abigail's Party', opened at the Hampstead Theatre starring Alison Steadman.

1978 The Andrew Lloyd Webber musical 'Evita' opens in London.
The arcade video game, 'Space Invaders' is released.

1979 Margaret Thatcher opens the new Central Milton Keynes Shopping Centre, the largest indoor shopping centre in Britain.
Anthony Blunt, British art historian and former Surveyor of the Queen's Pictures, in exposed as a double agent for the Soviets during WW2.
The Sony Walkman, portable cassette player is released.

Pavarotti at the Met.

It was in his third season at the Metropolitan Opera House in New York that Luciano Pavarotti, the operatic tenor, would skyrocket to stardom. The company imported Covent Garden's production of Donizetti's *La Fille du Régiment* in 1972 as a vehicle for Joan Sutherland. The great Australian diva enjoyed a huge triumph, but the surprise for the audience was the young Italian tenor by her side who shared an equal part in the phenomenal success. This was the historic first Met performance telecast live on PBS as part of the long-running series that continues to the present day.

The Terracotta Army

'The Qin Tomb Terracotta Warriors and Horses' was constructed between 246-206BC as an afterlife guard for China's First Emperor, Qin Shihuang, from whom, China gets its name. He ordered it built to remember the army he led to triumph over other warring states, and to unite China.

The tomb and the army were all made by hand by some 700,000 artisans and labourers, and comprises thousands of life-size soldiers, each with different facial features and expressions, clothing, hairstyles and gestures, arranged in battle array.

All figures face east, towards the ancient enemies of Qin State, in rectangular formations and three separate vaults include rows of kneeling and standing archers, chariot war configurations and mixed forces of infantry, horse drawn chariots plus numerous soldiers armed with long spears, daggers and halberds.

FILMS

1970 - 1974

1970 Love Story, was the biggest grossing film a sentimental, tearjerker with the oft-quoted tagline, "Love means never having to say you're sorry." Nominated for the Academy Awards Best Picture, it was beaten by **Patton** which won 7 major titles that year.

1971 The Oscar winner was **The French Connection** with Gene Hackman as a New York police detective, Jimmy 'Popeye' Doyle, chasing down drug smugglers. Hackman was at the peak of his career in the 70's.

1972 Francis Ford Coppola's gangster saga, **The Godfather** became the highest grossing film of its time and helped drive a resurgence in the American film industry.

1973 Glenda Jackson won Best Actress for her role in **A Touch of Class.** She revealed that she was approached for the part by the director after appearing in the 1971 'Antony & Cleopatra' sketch on the Morecambe & Wise show. After she won, Eric Morecambe sent her a telegram saying, "Stick with us and we will get you another one".

1974 New films this year included **The Godfather Part II,** which won the Oscar, **Blazing Saddles** the comedy western and the disaster film, **The Towering Inferno** starring Paul Newman and Steve McQueen.

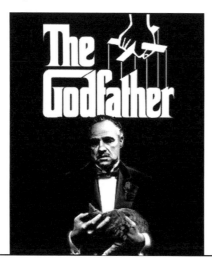

1975 - 1979

1975 One Flew Over the Cuckoo's Nest, an allegorical film set in a mental hospital, starring Jack Nicholson, beat tough competition for Best Picture from Spielberg's **Jaws** and Altman's **Nashville.**

1976 Jodi Foster won an Oscar in Martin Scorsese's gritty film **Taxi Driver** which examines alienation in urban society but it was Sylvester Stallone's **Rocky** that carried off the Best Picture award.

1977 Annie Hall from Woody Allen, the winner of Best Picture is a masterpiece of witty and quotable one-liners.

1978 The Vietnam War is examined through the lives of three friends from a small steel-mill town before, during and after their service in **The Deer Hunter**. A powerful and disturbing film.

1979 In this year's Best Picture, **Kramer v Kramer** there is a restaurant scene where Dustin Hoffman throws his wine glass at the wall. Only the cameraman was forewarned, Meryl Streep's shocked reaction was genuine!

IN THE 1970S

Star Wars

Star Wars all began with George Lucas's eponymous film in 1977. The epic space fantasy, telling the adventures of characters "A long time ago in a galaxy far, far away", and this first film was a world beater in special effects technology using new computerised and digital effects. It rapidly became a phenomenon, Luke Skywalker, Jedi Knights, Princess Leia and Darth Vader becoming household names. An immensely valuable franchise grew up to include the films, television series, video games, books, comics and theme parks which now amounts to billions of dollars and the film introduced the phrase "May the Force be with you" into common usage.

Apocalypse Now

Joseph Conrad's book 'Heart of Darkness' was the inspiration for producer and director Francis Ford Coppola's psychological film, a metaphor for the madness and folly of war itself for a generation of young American men. Beautiful, with symbolic shots showing the confusion, violence and fear of the nightmare of the Vietnam War, much of it was filmed on location in the Philippines where expensive sets were destroyed by severe weather, a typhoon called 'Olga', Marlon Brando showed up on set overweight and completely unprepared and Martin Sheen had a near-fatal heart attack.

This led to the film being two and a half times over budget and taking twice the number of scheduled weeks to shoot. When filming finally finished, the release was postponed several times as Coppola had six hours of film to edit. The helicopter attack scene with the 'Ride of the Valkyries' soundtrack is one of the most memorable film scenes ever.

Women Wear the Trousers

It is often said that 1970s styles had no direction and were too prolific. French couture no longer handed down diktats of what we should be wearing, and the emerging street style was inventive, comfortable, practical for women or glamorous. It could be home-made, it was whatever you wanted it to be, and the big new trend was for gender neutral clothes, women wore trousers in every walk of life, trouser suits for the office, jeans at home and colourful, tight-fitting ones for in between. Trouser legs became wider and 'bell-bottoms', flared from the knee down, with bottom leg openings of up to twenty-six inches, made from denim, bright cotton and satin polyester, became mainstream. Increasingly 'low cut', they were teamed with platform soles or high cut boots until they could not flare anymore, and so, by the end of the decade they had gone, skin-tight trousers, in earth tones, greys, whites and blacks were much more in vogue.

And the Hot Pants

In the early 70s, women's styles were very flamboyant with extremely bright colours and, in the winter, long, flowing skirts and trousers *but* come the summer, come the Hot Pants. These extremely short shorts were made of luxury fabrics such as velvet and satin designed for fashionable wear, not the practical equivalents for sports or leisure, and they enjoyed great popularity until falling out of fashion in the middle of the decade. Teamed with skin-tight t-shirts, they were favourites for clubwear and principally worn by women, including Jacqueline Kennedy Onassis, Elizabeth Taylor and Jane Fonda, but they were also worn by some high-profile men, David Bowie, Sammy Davis Jnr and Liberace among them, although the shorts were slightly longer than the women's versions, but still shorter than usual. Chest hair, medallions, sideburns and strangely, tennis headbands, finished the look!

These Boots Are Made For Walking

Boots were so popular in the early 1970s that even men were getting in on the action. It wasn't uncommon to see a man sporting 2" inch platform boots inspired by John Travolta in Saturday Night Fever. The trend was all about being sexy on the dance floor!

And Punk Was Not to Be Ignored

Emerging in the mid 70s in London as an anarchic and aggressive movement, a few hundred young people defined themselves as an anti-fashion urban youth street culture closely aligned to the music that became punk. They cut up old clothes from charity shops, destroyed the fabric and refashioned outfits in a manner intended to shock. Trousers were deliberately torn to reveal laddered tights and dirty legs and worn with heavy Doc Martens footwear, now seen on many young women too.

Safety pins and chains held bits of fabric together. Neck chains were made from padlocks and chain and even razor blades were used as pendants. Body piercings and studs, beginning with the three-stud earlobe, progressing to the ear outline embedded with ear studs, evolved to pins in eyebrows, cheeks, noses or lips and together with tattoos were the beginning of unisex fashion. All employed by male and female alike to offend. Vivienne Westwood and Malcolm McLaren quickened the style with her bondage shop "Sex", and his punk music group, the "Sex Pistols".

SATURDAY MORNING TV

In the early 70s, Saturday mornings for many children still meant a trip to the cinema but with the advent of Saturday Morning Television, under instruction 'not to wake their parents', children could creep downstairs, switch on the box and stay entertained until lunchtime.

First, in 1974, came ITV's 'Tiswas', hosted by Chris Tarrant it was a chaotic blend of jokes, custard pies and buckets of water.

Then in 1976, the BBC introduced 'Swap Shop' with Noel Edmonds, Keith Chegwin and John Craven and a Saturday morning ritual was born. Nearly three hours of ground-breaking television using the 'phone-in' extensively for the first time on TV. The programme included music, competitions, cartoons and spontaneous nonsense from Edmonds. There was coverage of news and issues relevant to children, presented by 'Newsround's' John Craven but by far the most popular element of the show was the "Swaporama" open-air event, hosted by Chegwin. An outside broadcast unit would travel to different locations throughout the UK where sometimes as many as 2000 children would gather to swap their belongings with others.

SATURDAY NIGHT FEVER

Memories of Saturday night and Sunday morning in the discotheque. A mirror ball; strobe lights; 'four on the floor' rhythm; the throb of the bass drum; girls in Spandex tops with hot pants or vividly coloured, shiny, Lycra trousers with equally dazzling halter neck tops; boys in imitations of John Travolta's white suit from Saturday Night Fever risking life and limb on towering platform shoes.

These glamorous dancers, clad in glitter, metallic lame and sequins, gyrating as the music pounded out at the direction of the DJ, whirling energetically and glowing bright 'blue-white' under the ultra-violet lights as their owners 'strutted their stuff', perspiration running in rivulets down their backs.

The DJs, stars in their own right, mixed tracks by Donna Summer, the Bee Gees, Gloria Gaynor, Sister Sledge, Chic and Chaka Khan, as their sexy followers, fuelled by the night club culture of alcohol and drugs, changed from dancing the Hustle with their partners to the solo freestyle dancing of John Travolta.

The Dangers of Leisure

In the 1970's the Government was intent on keeping us all – and particularly children – safe and continued producing the wartime Public Information Films, which were still scaring children witless!

1971: Children and Disused Fridges: Graphic warnings of children being suffocated in old fridges that, tempted by their playful imaginations, they want to climb into.

1973: Broken Glass: This film shows a boy running on the sand, ending abruptly before he steps on a broken glass bottle, the film urges people to use a bin or take their litter home with them.

1974: The Fatal Floor: This 30 second film had the message, "Polish a floor, put a rug on it, and you might as well set a man trap…"

1979: Play Safe – Frisbee: This film used chilling electronic music and frightening sound effects to highlight the potentially fatal combination of frisbees with electricity pylons and kites, fishing rods and radio-controlled planes.

1972: Teenagers – Learn to Swim:

A cartoon aimed at teenagers warns them to learn how to swim, or risk social embarrassment and failure to attract the opposite sex. The female character's illusion of her boyfriend 'Dave' being able 'to do anything' is shattered after she wishes they were at the seaside, where she discovers Dave can't swim. He in turn wishes he didn't 'keep losing me birds' after his girlfriend disappears with 'Mike' who 'swims like a fish'. Although the film is light-hearted in tone it was intended in part to help prevent accidents.

1975: Protect and Survive:

This was the title of a series of booklets and films made in the late 1970s and early 1980s, dealing with emergency planning for a nuclear war including the recognition of attack warning, fallout warning, and all-clear signals, the preparation of a home "fallout room" and the stockpiling of food, water, and other emergency supplies. In the opinion of some contemporary critics, the films *were deeply and surprisingly fatalistic in tone*!

1970 - 1974

1970 Number 1 for 3 weeks, **Bridge Over Troubled Water** by Simon and Garfunkel became their 'signature song' selling over 6m copies worldwide. It also became one of the most performed songs of the 20th century, covered by over 50 artists.

1971 George Harrison's first release as a solo **My Sweet Lord** topped the charts for five weeks and became the best selling UK single of the year.
Rod Stewart had 7 No 1's this year including in October, the double sided hits, **Reason to Believe/Maggie May**

1972 A jingle, rewritten to become the hugely popular 'Buy the world a Coke' advert for the Coca Cola company, was re-recorded by The New Seekers as the full-length song, **I'd Like to Teach the World to Sing**, which stayed at No 1 for 4 weeks.

1973 Dawn featuring Tony Orlando had the bestselling single of 1973 with **"Tie a Yellow Ribbon Round the 'Ole Oak Tree"**, which spent four weeks at the top spot and lasted 11 weeks in the top ten.
Queen released their debut album, **"Queen"**. The Carpenters reached number 2 with **"Yesterday Once More"**.

1974 Waterloo, the winning song for Sweden in the Eurovision Song Contest began ABBA's journey to world-wide fame.
David Essex has his first No 1 with **Wanna Make You a Star** which spends 3 weeks at the top of the charts.

1975 - 1979

1975 Make Me Smile (Come Up and See Me) was a chart topper for Steve Harley & Cockney Rebel. **Bohemian Rhapsody** for Queen, stayed at the top for nine weeks.

1976 The Brotherhood of Man won the Eurovision Song Contest for Great Britain with **Save Your Kisses for Me**. It became the biggest-selling song of the year and remains one of the biggest-selling Eurovision winners ever.
Don't Go Breaking My Heart was the first No. 1 single in the UK for both Elton John and Kiki Dee.

1977 Actor David Soul, riding high on his success in Starsky & Hutch, had the No 1 spot for 4 weeks with **Don't Give Up on Us**.
Way Down was the last song to be recorded by Elvis Presley before his death and stayed at No 1 for 5 weeks.

1978 Kate Bush released her debut single, **Wuthering Heights,** which she had written aged 18 after watching Emily Brontë's Wuthering Heights on television and discovering she shared the author's birthday.
Spending five weeks at the top of the British charts, Boney M's **"Rivers of Babylon"** became the biggest selling single of the year, exceeding one million sales between May and June.

1979 Frequently recalled as a symbol of female empowerment, **I Will Surviv**e reached the top for Gloria Gaynor.
The Wall, Pink Floyd's rock opera was released, featuring all three parts of **Another Brick in the Wall. Part 2**, written as a protest against rigid schooling was No1 in Dec.

In The 1970s

The Decade in Numbers

Most No1 Singles:
ABBA with seven.
Waterloo (1974);
Mamma Mia, Fernando
and
Dancing Queen (all 1976);
Knowing Me Knowing You,
The Name of the Game,
(both 1977);
Take a Chance on Me
(1978).

Most Weeks at No 1:
Bohemian Rhapsody by
Queen; **Mull of Kintyre /**
Girl's School by Wings;
You're the One That I Want
by John Travolta and Olivia
Newton-John.

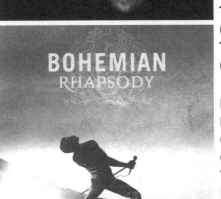

'Danny' and 'Sandy' Fever

Grease, the 1978 musical romantic comedy starring John Travolta (Danny) and Olivia Newton-John (Sandy) had phenomenal success. In June to August 1978, **You're the One That I Want** and in September to October, **Summer Nights**, locked up the number 1 position for a total of sixteen weeks.

Hopelessly Devoted to You was nominated for an Oscar and John Travolta and Olivia Newton-John seemed to be constantly in the public conscience. Critically and commercially successful, the soundtrack album ended 1978 as the second best-selling album in the US, behind the soundtrack of the 1977 blockbuster **Saturday Night Fever,** which also starred John Travolta.

43

Pocket Calculators

The first pocket calculators came onto the market towards the end of 1970. In the early 70s they were an expensive status symbol but by the middle of the decade, businessmen were quite used to working their sales figures out quickly whilst 'out of the office'.

Household accounts were made easy and children wished they could use them at school – not just to help with homework. Most early calculators performed only basic addition, subtraction, multiplication and division but the speed and accuracy, sometimes giving up to 12 digit answers, of the machine proved sensational.

In 1972, Hewlett Packard introduced the revolutionary HP-35 pocket calculator which, in addition to the basic operations, enabled advanced mathematical functions. It was the first scientific, hand-held calculator, able to perform a wide number of logarithmic and trigonometric functions, store intermediate solutions and utilise scientific notations.

With intense competition, prices of pocket calculators dropped rapidly, and the race was on to produce the smallest possible models. The target was to be no bigger than a credit card. Casio won the race.

The Miracle of IVF

In 1971, Patrick Steptoe, gynaecologist, Robert Edwards, biologist, and Jean Purdy, nurse and embryologist set up a small laboratory at the Kershaw's Hospice in Oldham which was to lead to the development of in vitro fertilisation and eventual birth of Louise Brown in 1978.

They developed a technique for retrieving eggs at the right time and fertilising them in the laboratory, believing that they could be implanted back in the uterus. It took more than 80 embryo transfers before the first successful pregnancy, and the birth of Louise, the first 'test-tube baby', heralded the potential happiness of infertile people and a bright future for British science and industry. 8

IN THE 1970S

"Houston We Have a Problem"

In April 1970, two days after the launch of Apollo 13, the seventh crewed mission in the Apollo space program and the third meant to land on the Moon, the NASA ground crew heard the now famous message, "Houston, we've had a problem." An oxygen tank had exploded, and the lunar landing was aborted leaving the astronauts in serious danger. The crew looped around the Moon and returned safely to Earth, their safe return being down to the ingenuity under pressure by the crew, commanded by Jim Lovell, together with the flight controllers and mission control. The crew experienced great hardship, caused by limited power, a chilly and wet cabin and a shortage of drinking water.

Even so, Apollo 13 set a spaceflight record for the furthest humans have travelled from Earth.

Tens of millions of viewers watched Apollo 13 splashdown in the South Pacific Ocean and the recovery by USS Iwo Jima.

The global campaigning network **Greenpeace** was founded in 1971 by Irving and Dorothy Stowe, environmental activists. The network now has 26 independent national or regional organisations in 55 countries worldwide.

Their stated goal is to ensure the ability of the earth to nurture life in all its diversity. To achieve this they "use non-violent, creative confrontation to expose global environmental problems, and develop solutions for a green and peaceful future". In detail to:

- Stop the planet from warming beyond 1.5° in order to prevent the most catastrophic impacts of the climate breakdown.
- Protect biodiversity in all its forms.
- Slow the volume of hyper-consumption and learn to live within our means.
- Promote renewable energy as a solution that can power the world.
- Nurture peace, global disarmament and non-violence.

1970 - 1974

1970 The thoroughbred 'Nijinsky', wins all three English Triple Crown Races: **The 2,000 Guineas** at Newmarket; **The Derby** at Epsom; the **St. Leger Stakes** at Doncaster and the Irish Derby. The first horse to do this in 35 years and not repeated as of 2021.

1971 Arsenal wins both the **First Division** title and the **FA Cup**, becoming the fourth team ever to win the double.
Jack Nicklaus wins his ninth major at the **PGA Championship**, the first golfer ever to win all four majors for the second time.

1972 At **Wimbledon**, Stan Smith (US) beat Ilie Nastase in the Men's Singles Final. It was his only Wimbledon title.
In the Women's Final, Billie Jean King (US) beat Yvonne Goolagong (AUS) to gain her fourth **Wimbledon** title.
The **Olympic Games** held in Munich are overshadowed by the murder of eleven Israeli athletes and coaches by Palestinian Black September members.

1973 George Foreman knocks out Joe Frazier in only two rounds to take the **World Heavyweight Boxing** Championship title.

Red Rum wins the **Grand National** with a new record and staging a spectacular comeback on the run-in having trailed the leader by 15 lengths at the final fence.

1974 Liverpool win the **FA Cup Final** against Newcastle United at Wembley. Kevin Keegan scored two of their three goals.
Eddie Merckx wins the **Tour de France**, becoming the first rider to win the Triple Crown of Cycling, **Tour de France**, **Giro d'Italia** and **World Championships** in one calendar year.

1975 - 1979

1975 In athletics, John Walker (NZ) sets a new world record becoming the first man to **run a mile** in under 3 mins 50 seconds. He clocks 3mins 49.4 secs.
Muhammad Ali defeats Joe Frazier in the 'Thrilla In Manilla' to maintain the **Boxing Heavyweight Championship** of the world.

1976 The **Olympics** are held in Montreal. Britain's only medal is a Bronze, won by Brendan Foster running the **10,000 metres**.
John Curry, becomes the **European, Olympic and World Figure Skating Champion**. He was the first skater to combine, ballet and modern dance into his skating.

1977 The commercial **World Series Cricket** was introduced by Kerry Packer. WSC changed the nature of the game with its emphasis on the "gladiatorial" aspect of fast bowling and heavy promotion of fast bowlers.

1978 During the **Oxford and Cambridge Boat Race,** the Cambridge boat sinks. It is the first sinking in the race since 1951.
Wales wins the rugby **Five Nations Championship** and completes the Grand Slam having beaten England, France, Ireland and Scotland.

1978 Arsenal beat Manchester United 3-2 in the **FA Cup Final.**
At **The Open** at Royal Lytham & St Annes Golf Club Seve Ballesteros becomes the first golfer from Continental Europe to win a major since 1907.

Traffic Lights and Football

Before the introduction of Red and Yellow Cards in football, cautions or sending a player off had to be dealt with orally, and the language barrier could sometimes present problems. For example, in the 1966 World Cup, the German referee tried in vain to send Argentinian player Antonio Rattin off the field, but Rattin did not 'want' to understand and eventually was escorted off the pitch by the police! Ken Aston, Head of World Cup Referees, was tasked with solving this problem and legend has it that the idea of the red and yellow cards came to him when he was stopped in his car at traffic lights. They were tested in the 1968 Olympics and the 1970 World Cup in Mexico and introduced to European leagues soon after and after six years, to English football.

In 1976, the first player to be sent off using a red card in an English game was Blackburn Rovers winger David Wagstaffe.

Tour de France

In 1974 the Tour de France covered 2,546 miles in 22 stages, one of which was the first to be held in the UK, a circuit stage on the Plympton By-pass near Plymouth. Eddy Merckx of Belgium won eight stages and won the race overall with a comfortable margin, making it five wins for him out of his five Tours. He also won that year's Combination Classification – the General (Yellow Jersey), Points or Sprint (Green Jersey) and Mountains (since 1975, King of the Mountains wears the Polka Dot Jersey).

Rockstar and Racing Driver

James Hunt, the charismatic, play-boy darling of the press in the 1970's, began his Formula 1 career at the beginning of the decade with the Hesketh Racing team and gave them their only win in 1975 at the Dutch GP. He moved to McLaren in 1976, and in his first year with them, he and his great rival Niki Lauda at Ferrari, fought an epic season-long battle. It was an extraordinarily dramatic season, over sixteen races filled with drama and controversy, where Lauda had gained an early championship lead. By the final race in Japan, he was being reeled-in by Hunt and was only three points ahead. Hunt drove the race of his life, in the worst possible weather conditions, to finish in third place. Lauda, already badly injured from the crash at Nürburgring in August, withdrew because of the hazardous conditions which meant James Hunt became World Champion, winning by just a single point.

Hunt's natural driving ability was phenomenal, and while his habit of risk-taking didn't always endear him to others, hence the nickname "Hunt the Shunt", it also made him compelling to watch. Off track, he and Niki had an enduring friendship, which lasted after James's retirement from F1 in 1979 until his untimely death from a heart attack in 1993, aged just 45.

ICONIC MACHINES OF THE DECADE

The Jumbo Jet
Entered service on January 22, 1970. The 747 was the first airplane dubbed a "Jumbo Jet", the first wide-body airliner.

In 1971 Ford launched the car that was to represent the 1970s, the Cortina Mk III. In 1976 the Mk IV and 1979 Mk V. Cortinas were the best-selling cars of the decade.

The best-selling foreign import was the Datsun Sunny, which was only the 19th best-selling car of the decade.

In 1973, British Leyland's round, dumpy shaped Allegro was not at all popular and meagre sales contributed greatly to BL's collapse in 1975.

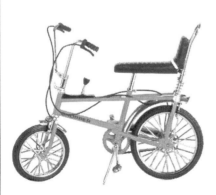

Raleigh Chopper
Shot to fame in the 70's when every child, and some adults, wanted one. It had a high back, long seat and motorbike rear wheel and was probably the first bike to have a centrally positioned gear shift.

Women Drivers

In 1974, Jill Viner became the first female bus driver for London Transport. She trained to become a bus driver at a centre in Chiswick in 1974, when London Transport were said to be 3,200 drivers short

While women had previously driven buses within bus depots during the Second World War, Viner was the first women to drive a bus in service in London. In the weeks after she started driving, it was reported that thirty women had applied to become bus drivers.

In 1978, Hannah Dadds completed a seven-week training course to qualify as a train driver and became the first female driver on the London Underground.

Hannah's sister Edna also joined the London Underground working first as a guard and then a driver. Hannah and Edna became the first all-female crew on the London Underground.

Concorde

The Anglo-French supersonic passenger airliner had a take-off speed of 220 knots (250mph) and a cruising speed of 1350mph – more than twice the speed of sound. With seating for 92 to 128 passengers, Concorde entered service in 1976 and operated for 27 years.

Twenty aircraft were built in total, including six prototypes and in the end, only Air France and British Airways purchased and flew them, due in great part to supersonic flights being restricted to ocean-crossing routes, to prevent sonic boom disturbance over land and populated areas. Concorde flew regular transatlantic flights from London and Paris to New York, Washington, Dulles in Virginia and Barbados and the BA Concorde made just under 50,000 flights and flew more than 2.5m passengers supersonically.

A typical London to New York crossing would take a little less than three and a half hours as opposed to about eight hours for a subsonic flight.

The aircraft was retired in 2003, three years after the crash of an Air France flight in which all passengers and crew were killed.

THE MAJOR NEWS STORIES

1980 - 1984

1980:

May: Mount St. Helens experiences a huge eruption that creates avalanches, explosions, large ash clouds, mudslides, and massive damage. 57 people are killed.

Dec: John Lennon, the former Beatle, age 40, is shot and killed by an obsessed fan in Manhattan.

1981:

July: Prince Charles marries Lady Diana Spencer at St Paul's Cathedral.

Margaret Thatcher's Government begins the privatisation of the Nationalised Industries.

1982:

Apr: Argentina invades the Falkland Islands and the UK retakes possession of them by the end of June.

May: Pope John Paul II visits the United Kingdom. It is the first visit by a reigning Pope

1983:

Apr: The £1 coin is introduced in the UK.

Jun: Margaret Thatcher wins a landslide victory for the Conservatives in the General Election, with a majority of 144.

Nov: The first United States cruise missiles arrive at RAF Greenham Common in Berkshire

1984:

Mar: The National Mineworkers Union led by Arthur Scargill, begin what will be a year-long strike against the National Coal Board's plans to shut 20 collieries

May: The Thames Barrier, designed to protect London from floods, is opened by9The Queen

1980: Mount St. Helens before and after the eruption. The top third of the mountain was blown away.

1982: EPCOT opened at Disney World in Florida, "...an experimental prototype community of tomorrow that will take its cue from the new ideas and technologies that are now emerging ... a showcase of the ingenuity and imagination of American free enterprise." - *Walt Disney*

1984: On 31 October, Indira Gandhi, Prime Minister of India, was killed by her Sikh bodyguards.
The assassination sparked four days of riots that left more than 8,000 Indian Sikhs dead in revenge attacks.

IN THE 1980s

You cannot be serious!

During the 1981 Wimbledon Championships, John McEnroe uttered what has become the most immortal phrase in tennis, if not all sport, when he screamed "you cannot be serious" at a Wimbledon umpire while disputing a line call. Already called "Superbrat" by the British tabloid press for his verbal volleys during previous Wimbledon matches, it was in a first-round match against fellow American Tom Gullikson, who was serving at 15-30 and 1-1 in the first set when a McEnroe shot was called out. Approaching the umpire, he said: "Chalk came up all over the place, you can't be serious man." Then, his anger rising, he bawled the words that would stay with him for a lifetime and find its way into the sporting annals. "You cannot be serious," he screamed. "That ball was on the line".

On the receiving end of the tirade was umpire Edward James, who eventually responded by politely announcing: "I'm going to award a point against you Mr McEnroe." It made little difference, McEnroe went on to win in straight sets and two weeks later had his final victory over Bjorn Borg.

Torvill and Dean

On Valentine's Day 1984, Jayne Torvill and Christopher Dean made history at the Winter Olympics in Sarajevo and set a new standard for world class figure skating. The duo from Nottingham, were the last to perform in their category and their performance, self-choreographed to 4½ minutes of Ravel's Bolero, was seamless, elegant and hypnotic. As they sank to the ice in the dramatic finale, the whole stadium stood and applauded. Their dance had captured the world's imagination and won Gold. The unanimous scores of 6.0 for artistic impression made them the highest-scoring figure skaters of all time.

Their routine, made Ravel's Boléro with its steady crescendo and repeated snare-drum rhythms, synonymous with figure-skating.

TRANSPORT

British Car Manufacturing

Gallery:

The 1980s was still a busy period for British car manufacturers and many of the bestselling cars of the decade were made in Britain.

The top 10 cars were:
1. Ford Escort
2. Vauxhall Cavalier
3. Ford Fiesta
4. Austin Metro
5. Ford Sierra (which replaced the
6. Ford Cortina)
6. Vauxhall Astra
7. Ford Orion
8. Austin Maestro
9. Vauxhall Nova
10. Ford Grenada

However the list of the **'Most influential Cars of the 1980s'** shows how the British car industry was soon to be decimated. The list includes:

Audi Quatrro; Porsche 944: Renault Scenic; Mercedes 190; BMW 3 Series; VW Golf; Volvo 240 Estate; Peugeot 205 and the Toyota Carolla.

The Ford Cortina was replaced by the Ford Sierra in 1982

The Ford Fiesta has been ever popular right up to the present day.

The Austin Metro was the replacement for the mini.

The VW Golf had front wheel drive and built a reputation for quality and reliability

The Porsche 944 was the choice of the newly rich 'yuppies' of the 1980s

Clunk Click Every Trip

Although car manufacturers had been obliged to install seatbelts since 1965, it was not until January 1983 that the law requiring all drivers to wear their belts came into force. In spite of a great deal of 'grumbling' and more, ranging from *"the erosion of our civil liberties, another example of the Nanny State"*, to *"its uncomfortable, restrictive and creases my clothes"* and horror stories of crash victims being *"hanged"* by their belts or suffering greater injury, 90% of drivers and front seat passengers were observed to be wearing seat belts soon after the law came into effect – and these rates have been sustained since then. There was an immediate 25% reduction in driver fatalities and a 29 per cent reduction in fatal injuries among front seat passengers.

In 1989 it became compulsory for all children under 14 to wear a seat belt in the rear and when seatbelt wearing became compulsory for all rear-seat occupants in 1991, there was an immediate increase from 10% to 40% in observed seat belt wearing rates.

Aviation

When Airbus designed the A300 during the late 1960s and early 1970s, it envisaged a broad family of airliners with which to compete against Boeing and Douglas, the two established US aerospace manufacturers.

The launch of the A320 in 1987 guaranteed the status of Airbus as a major player in the aircraft market – the aircraft had over 400 orders before it first flew.

Motorcycles

Only 3000 Honda FVR750R motorcycles were made, race bred machines with lights thrown on to make them road legal and sold to the public. The first batch of 1000 sold out instantly. With a top speed of 153mph the V-four powered RC30 was one of the fastest sports bike of the decade but it was the track proven frame that meant it handled like a genuine racer. It also had a soundtrack to die for and was absolutely beautiful.

The Docklands Light Railway

The Docklands Light Railway was first opened in August 1987 as an automated, light metro system to serve the redeveloped Docklands area of London as a cheap public transport solution. The original network comprised two routes - Tower Gateway to Island Gardens and Stratford to Island Gardens and was mainly elevated on disused railway viaducts, new concrete viaducts and disused surface railway tracks. The trains were fully automated, controlled by computer, and had no driver.

They did however have a "Train Captain" who was responsible for patrolling the train, checking tickets, making announcements and controlling the doors. They could take control of the train should there be an equipment failure or emergency. The first generation of rolling stock comprised eleven lightweight units and the stations, mostly of a common design, constructed from standard components and usually featuring a short half-cylindrical, glazed, blue canopy, were designed specifically for these single articulated trains. The 15 stations were all above ground and needed no staff.

THE MAJOR NEWS STORIES

1990 - 1994

1990:
Feb: Nelson Mandela is released from prison in South Africa, after 27 years behind bars.

Nov: Margaret Thatcher resigns as Prime Minister. At 11 years, she was the longest serving PM of the 20th Century.

1991:
Jan: The Gulf War begins, as the Royal Air Force joins Allied aircraft in bombing raids on Iraq

Apr: After a year of protests and riots, the government confirms that the Poll Tax is to be replaced by a new Council Tax in 1993.

1992:
Apr: At the General Election the Conservative Party are re-elected for a fourth term under John Major.

Nov: Part of Windsor Castle is gutted in a fire causing millions of pounds worth of damage and The Queen describes this year as an Annus Horribilis.

1993:
Apr: The Queen announces that Buckingham Palace will open to the public for the first time

Sep: The UK Independence Party which supports the breakaway from the EU is formed.

Dec: Diana, Princess of Wales. withdraws from public life.

1994:
Mar: The Church of England ordains its first female priests.

May: The Channel Tunnel between Britain and France is officially opened.

Nov: The first UK National Lottery draw takes place.

1992: The 'Maastricht Treaty' was concluded between the 'then' twelve member states of the European Communities. This foundation treaty of the EU announced a new stage in the process of European integration, shared citizenship and a single currency. There were two headquarters, one in Brussels and one in Strasbourg,

1991: The internet already existed but no one had thought of a way of how to link one document directly to another until in 1989, British scientist Tim Berners-Lee, invented the WorldWideWeb. The www. was introduced in 1991 as the first web browser and the first website went online in August.

1997: The UK transfers sovereignty of Hong Kong, the largest remaining British colony, to the People's Republic of China as the 99 years lease on the territory formally ends.

1999: On 1st January, the new European currency, the Euro is launched and some 320 million people from eleven European countries begin carrying the same money in their wallets.
Britain's Labour government preferred to stay with the pound sterling instead.

1995 - 1999

1995:
Feb: Barings Bank, the UK's oldest merchant bank, collapses after rogue trader Nick Leeson loses $1.4 billion.

Apr: All telephone area dialling codes are changed in the UK.

Aug: Pubs in England are permitted to remain open throughout Sunday afternoon.

1996:
Feb: The Prince and Princess of Wales agree to divorce more than three years after separating.

Jul: Dolly the Sheep becomes the first mammal to be successfully cloned from an adult cell.

1997:
May: Tony Blair wins a landslide General Election for the Labour Party.

Aug: Princess Diana is killed in a car crash in Paris. Dodi Fayed, the heir to the Harrods empire is killed with her

1998:
Mar: Construction on the Millenium Dome begins. It will be the centre piece for a national celebration.

Apr: The Good Friday Agreement between the UK and Irish governments is signed.

1999:
Apr: A minimum wage is introduced in the UK – set at £3.60 an hour for workers over 21, and £3 for workers under 21

Jun: Construction of the Millenium Dome is finished and in October, the London Eye begins to be lifted into position.

Home life in the 1990s was changing again. Family time was not cherished as it had once been, children had a lot more choice and were becoming more independent with their own TVs programmes, personal computers, music systems, mobile phones and, crucially, the introduction of the world wide web, which meant life would never be the same again.

After school and weekend organised activities for the young burgeoned, with teenagers able to take advantage of the fast-food chains, or eating at different times, meaning no more family eating together. Families 'lived in separate' rooms, there were often two televisions so different channels could be watched and children wanted to play with their Nintendos or listen to their Walkmans in their own rooms. Their rooms were increasingly themed, from Toy Story to Athena posters, a ceiling full of sticker stars that illuminated a room with their green glow and somewhere in the house, room had to be made for the computer desk.

Track lighting was an easy way to illuminate a room without relying on multiple lamps and it became a popular feature in many '90s homes along with corner baths — most of which also had a water jet function which suddenly turned your bath into a low-budget jacuzzi!

In 1990, 68% of UK households owned at least one car, and the use of 'out of town' supermarkets and shopping centres, where just about anything and everything could be purchased in the same area, meant that large weekly or even monthly shops could be done in a single outing and combined with the huge increase in domestic freezers and ready prepared foods, time spent in the kitchen and cooking could be greatly reduced.

Over 80% of households owned a washing machine and 50%, a tumble dryer, so the need to visit the laundrette all but disappeared and instead of "Monday is washing day", the family's laundry could be carried out on an 'as and when' basis. All contributing to an increase in leisure time.

Nearly three-quarters of homes had microwave cookers and for working women who did not want to do their own cleaning, Merry Maids set up their home cleaning franchise in the UK in 1990 and many other companies followed suit.

Commuting
In Great Britain at the beginning of the 1990s, the *average* one-way commute to work was 38 minutes in London, 33 minutes in the south-east, and 21 minutes in the rest of the country. By the end of the decade, full-time workers commuting to and from London, had lost an additional 70 minutes per week of home time to commuting but, by contrast, outside the south-east of Britain, there was no increase in commuting time over the decade. In the south-east, 30% of workers took at least 45 minutes to get to work. In the rest of the country, only 10% did.

ART AND CULTURE

1990 - 1994

1990 In Rome, on the eve of the final of the FIFA World Cup, the Three Tenors sing together for the first time. The event is broadcast live and watched worldwide by millions of people. The highlight is Luciano Pavarotti's performance of Nessun Dorma.

The first Hampton Court Palace Flower Show takes place.

1991 Dame Margot Fonteyn, the Royal Ballet's Prima Ballerina, dies in Panama City, exactly 29 years after her premiere with Rudolf Nureyev who made his debut in 'Giselle'.

1992 Damien Hirst's "Shark", featuring a preserved shark, is first shown at an exhibition at the Saatchi Gallery in London.

Under the new Further and Higher Education Act, Polytechnics are allowed to become new Universities and award degrees of their own.

The last edition of Punch, the UK's oldest satirical magazine since 1841, is published.

1993 Bookmakers cut their odds on the monarchy being abolished by the year 2000 from 100 to 1 to 50 to 1.

QVC launches the first television shopping channel in the UK.

1994 The Duchess of Kent joins the Roman Catholic Church, the first member of the Royal Family to convert to Catholicism for more than 300 years.

The Sunday Trading Act comes into full effect, permitting retailers to trade on Sundays but restricts larger stores to a maximum of six hours, between 10 am and 6 pm.

1995 - 1999

1995 The first ever World Book Day was held on 23rd April, picked to celebrate the anniversary of William Shakespeare's death.

The BBC begins regular Digital Audio Broadcasting from Crystal Palace.

1996 Shortly after publication of the Italian edition of his book 'The Art Forger's Handbook', English-born art forger, Eric Hebborn is beaten to death in Rome.

The Stone of Scone is installed in Edinburgh Castle 700 years after it was removed from Scotland by King Edward I of England.

1997 The Teletubbies caused a sensation when they appeared on BBC TV. They were the most sought-after toy of the year.

The reconstruction of the Elizabethan Globe Theatre, called Shakespeare's Globe opens in London with a production of Shakespeare's 'Henry V'.

1998 Britain's largest sculpture, the Angel of the North by Anthony Gormley is installed at Low Eighton, Gateshead.

More than 15,000 people attend a tribute concert held for Diana, Princess of Wales, at her family home, Althorp Park.

1999 The children's picture book, 'The Gruffalo' by Julia Donaldson is first published.

Media coverage for the Turner Prize was dominated by extreme critical response to Tracey Emin's work 'My Bed' – an installation of her unmade bed, complete with dirty sheets and detritus.

IN THE 1990S

1997: 'Harry Potter and the Philosopher's Stone' by JK Rowling made its debut in June. The initial edition of this first book in the series, comprised 500 copies and the novel has gone on to sell in excess of 120 million. The success of the whole Harry Potter phenomenon is well known, and there have been less expected benefits too. Certainly, before the films, children loved reading the books and boosted the reported numbers of children reading and indeed, reading longer books.

The perception of boarding schools, often associated with misery and cruel, spartan regimes was changed for some by Hogwarts School of Witchcraft and Wizardry. The sense of excitement, community and friendship of the children, the camaraderie of eating together and playing together, made going away to school more appealing for many.

The amazing visual effects used in the films were instrumental in persuading Hollywood to consider UK technical studios and raised the number of visual effects Oscar nominations for British companies significantly.

1997: The Guggenheim Museum of modern and contemporary art, designed by Canadian-American architect Frank Gehry, opened in Bilbao. The building represents an architectural landmark of innovating design, a spectacular structure.

The museum was originally a controversial project. Bilbao's industry, steel and shipbuilding was dying, and the city decided to regenerate to become a modern technological hub of the Basque region, and the controversy was, instead of an office block or factory, the centre piece would be a brand-new art gallery.

It is a spectacular building, more like a sculpture with twisted metal, glass, titanium and limestone, a futuristic setting for fine works of art. The gamble paid off, in the first twenty years, the museum attracted more than 19 million visitors with 70% from outside Spain. Foreign tourists continue to travel through the Basque country bringing a great economic boost to the region and Bilbao itself, has transformed from a grimy post-industrial town to a tourist hotspot.

FILMS

1990 - 1994

1990 It was Oscar time for an epic western this year and **Dances With Wolves**, directed and starring Kevin Costner with seven Academy Awards, won Best Picture and Best Director. It is one of only three Westerns to win the Oscar for Best Picture, the other two being **Cimmaron** in 1931 and **Unforgotten** in **1992**.

1991 *"Well, Clarice - have the lambs stopped screaming?"* wrote Dr Hannibal Lecter to the young FBI trainee, Clarice Starling. The thriller, **The Silence of the Lambs**, about a cannibalistic serial killer, scared audiences half to death and won the Best Picture Award.

1992 The nominations for the Academy Awards held some serious themes. **The Crying Game** was set against the backdrop of the 'troubles' in Northern Ireland. There was a blind retired Army officer in **Scent of a Woman**, rising troubles in colonial French Vietnam in **Indochine** and the invasion of Panama in **The Panama Deception**.

1993 The acclaimed **Schindler's List** won Best Picture with stiff competition from **The Piano** which won Best Original Screenplay and Robin Williams as **Mrs Doubtfire** which became the second highest grossing film of the year.

1994 Disney's animated musical **The Lion King** made the most money this year, but **Forest Gump** took the prize for Best Picture. The British film **Four Weddings and a Funeral** was a huge success and brought WH Auden's beautiful poem 'Funeral Blues' into the limelight.

1995 - 1999

1995 The tense, amazingly technically correct, story of the ill-fated **Apollo 13** quest to land on the moon failed to win the top Oscar, beaten by Mel Gibson in **Braveheart**, the American take on the story of William Wallace and the first Scottish war of independence against England.

1996 The English Patient a romantic war drama won the Best Picture, up against Mike Leigh's **Secrets and Lies** which won the Best British Film.

1997 The blockbuster **Titanic** was the film of the year. The combination of romance and disaster proving irresistible. Harland & Wolfe, the builders of RMS Titanic shared blueprints they thought were lost with the crew to produce the scale models, computer-generated imagery and a reconstruction of the ship itself, to re-create the sinking.

1998 Shakespeare in Love, a fictional love affair between Shakespeare and Viola de Lesseps whilst he is writing Romeo and Juliet was hugely popular and won seven Oscars.

1999 In **American Beauty,** Kevin Spacey plays Lester Burnham, an unhappy executive whose midlife awakening is the crux of the story. Bad as he thinks his life is, he cannot not stop seeing the beauty of the world around him.

**"Fear can hold you prisoner,
Hope can set you free."**

In 1994, Tim Robbins and Morgan Freeman starred **The Shawshank Redemption**, an inspirational, life-affirming and uplifting, old-fashioned style prison film and character study in the ilk of 'The Birdman of Alcatraz'. Set in a fictional, oppressive Shawshank State Prison in Maine, two imprisoned men bond over the years, in a tale of friendship, patience, hope, survival and ultimately finding solace and eventual redemption through acts of common decency.

The film was initially a box office disappointment. Many reasons were put forward for its failure at the time, including a general unpopularity of prison films, its lack of female characters and even the title, which was considered to be confusing. However, it was nominated for seven Academy Awards, failed to win a single Oscar, but this raised awareness and increased the film's popularity such that it is now preserved in the US National Film Registry as "culturally, historically, or aesthetically significant".

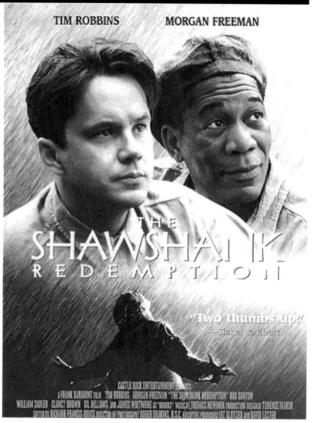

The Full Monty

In 1997 whilst huge audiences were crying over Kate Winslet and Leonardo di Caprio in **Titanic,** equally huge audiences were laughing at the story of six unemployed men in Sheffield, four of them former steel workers, who are in dire need of cash and who decide to emulate 'The Chippendales' dance, striptease troupe. They devise a dance act with their difference being, that Gaz decides their show must be even better than the originals and declares to the friends that they will go 'the full Monty' – they will strip all the way. Although primarily a comedy, the film touches on several serious subjects too, including unemployment, father's rights – Gaz is unable to pay maintenance to his estranged wife and she is seeking sole custody of his son – and working-class culture, depression and suicide. The film was a huge success as it ultimately is about humanity and the problems people all over the world struggle with.

SUPERMODELS

The original supermodels of the 1980s, Linda Evangelista, Naomi Campbell, Christy Turlington and Cindy Crawford were joined later by Claudia Schiffer and then Kate Moss to become the "Big Six". Models used to be categorised as 'print' or 'runway' but the "Big Six" showed that they could do it all, catwalk, print campaigns, magazine covers and even music videos and they became pop 'icons' in their own right. The models were also known for their earning capacity, one famous remark from Linda Evangelista, "We don't wake up for less than $10,000 a day!"

But with the popularity of grunge, came a shift away from the fashion for feminine curves and wholesome looking women, and in came the rise of a new breed of fragile, individual-looking and often younger, models, epitomised by Kate Moss. Her waif-like thinness and delicacy complemented the unkempt look that was popular in the early nineties and a new phrase 'heroin chic' described the down-at-heel settings for fashion shoots presented in magazines. By the end of the decade however, attitudes had shifted and concern about the health of the skeletal model was becoming a source of great debate.

GOTH

During the mid to late 1990s, the sub-culture of gothic fashion peaked in popularity. Their distinguishing features were black, antiquated and homogeneous features. Long black hair, black eyeliner, black nail polish, silver jewellery and face piercings teamed with long, black leather coats worn over frilly shirts and tight black trousers or even fetish wear. Girls often wore corsets, lace gloves and short leather skirts, velvets and fishnets with accessories often borrowed from the punk fashion such as spiked wristbands and chokers.

Siouxsie Sioux was particularly influential, since her gig at Futurama in 1980 she had been influencing how the music with the Banshees, would dress and she may well have been inspired by Theda Bara, the 1910s silent film, femme fatale, renowned for her dark eyeshadow and 'Vamp' look.

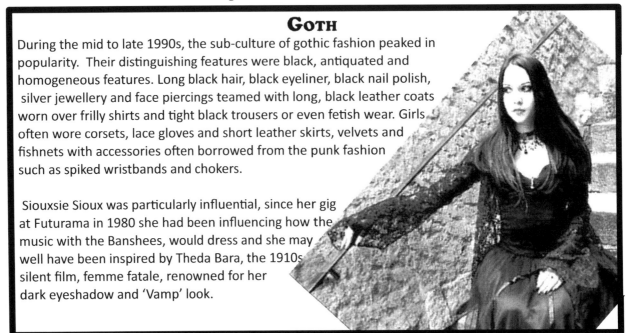

IN THE 1990S

GRUNGE

Grunge was a style for the young that emerged in Seattle in the late 1980s and by the early 90s had spread across the world. Made popular by bands such as Nirvana, it was a fashion for both men and women. The look was simple, an oversized flannel shirt, sometimes worn over a t-shirt, and baggy, worn out jeans to give an overall, dishevelled, appearance. The clothes were found ideally in charity shops or at the back of "Dad's wardrobe". A pair of Doc Martens or Converse shoes finished the ensemble.

Nirvana's lead singer Kurt Cobain epitomised the look with holes in his jeans and cardigan sweaters and the fashion world caught on when their second album, 'Nevermind' was released in 1991 and grunge made it onto the catwalk – specifically by Calvin Klein on an 18-year-old Kate Moss. Shrunken baby doll dresses, old prom dresses or even old petticoats and simple slip dresses appeared, often worn with chunky boots and for men, beanies, band t-shirts and knitted sweaters with patterns.

FRIENDS

For women, long loose hair was the most popular women's style, but the most requested hairstyle of the 1990s was said to be 'The Rachel'. Jennifer Anniston's character in 'Friends', Rachel Green, had the haircut people wanted – bouncy, layered, shoulder length, obviously styled to within an inch of its life yet at the same time artfully tousled.

HOODIES

Utilitarian styles such as cargo pants and The Gap's hooded sweatshirts became popular for everyday wear. Industrial and military styles crept into mainstream fashion and camouflage pants were everywhere on the street.
There was also a concerted move towards logoed clothing such as by Tommy Hilfiger

LEISURE

THE GAMES CHILDREN PLAYED

The trend in the 90s was for more electronic, video and computer games but younger children still enjoyed many of the traditional past-times, and events in the 90s such as the FIFA World Cups and the Olympics, produced special collections which reignited interest in collecting 'stickers,' and filling albums.

Crazes were still all the craze too and it was digital pets like Tamagotchi, housed in their small, egg-shaped, handheld video game console that became the biggest fads of the end of the decade.

The Teletubbies caused a huge sensation in 1997, communicating through gibberish and designed to resemble real-life toddlers, they became a huge commercial success, the toy Teletubbies being the most demanded toy of 1997.

However, it was Sony's PlayStation which was the big innovation of the 90s. The first version was able to process games stored on CD-ROMs and introduced 3D graphics to the industry. It had a low retail price and Sony employed aggressive youth marketing. Ridge Racer was the classic motor racing game used in the launch and the popularity of this game was crucial to the early success of the PlayStation.

RESTORATION OF THE SPA

From being at the centre of society in previous times, the spa industry had declined so much that by the 50s, leading spas such as those at Buxton, Cheltenham and Tunbridge Wells had closed. The 1990s saw a simultaneous rise of increasing disposable wealth, and the popularity of a new concept of the spa, pure self-indulgence and pampering.

The need to pause and detox from time to time fitted nicely into the growth of a 'wellness' culture and the understanding of holistic wellbeing, treatments to soothe the mind, body and spirit. Wearing a luxurious white robe and slippers, lounging by a heated pool reading magazines and dipping from time to time into the whirlpools, a trip to the steam room or sauna before taking a light lunch and then unwinding to a fragranced oil body massage because, as L'Oreal had been saying since the 70s, "you're worth it!"

In The 1990s

Where We Went on Holiday

In the 90s, if we went on a foreign holiday at all, 26m of us in 1996, the norm was to go for just the one, two-week summer break. Booking with a Travel Agent in town or finding a cheap package deal on Teletext, we arrived at our destination with a guide-book, Travellers Cheques and a camera complete with film.

Our favourite places were Spain and France, many of us travelling on the cross-Channel ferries rather than on the budget airlines. Our other favourite hot spots were Belgium, Turkey, Egypt, Kenya and Tunisia.

Although the gap year began in the 1960s, it was in the 1990s when the idea became the 'thing to do' amongst the children of the new wealthy middle classes.

Many visited India, Pakistan and Nepal, Australia, Thailand, the USA and New Zealand being their favoured countries to visit.

Some did voluntary work in the developing nations, building schools and teaching children English.

The 90s saw plenty of new cruise ships being launched for what became a massive growth industry. New cruise lines were formed, and many existing lines merged and Royal Caribbean, Celebrity, Fred Olsen and Carnival, Disney, Silver Sea and Princess lines were all introducing, predominantly older people, to new places and entertaining them royally on the way.

For others, at the opposite end of the cruising scale, was the immensely popular, 'Booze Cruise'. The day trip across the channel to France to stock up on duty free wine and cigarettes.

MUSIC

1990 - 1994

1990 Elton John's **Sacrifice** was initially released as a single in 1989 but only reached No. 55 in the UK. In mid-1990, Radio 1 DJ, Steve Wright began playing it and it soon caught on with other DJs and when re-released as a double A-side single with **Healing Hands** it became John's first solo No 1 single remaining at the top for five weeks.

1991 Cher made the 1960s **Shoop Shoop Song (It's in His Kiss)** an international hit once again. **(Everything I Do) I Do It for You**, from the soundtrack of the film 'Robin Hood: Prince of Thieves' was sung by Bryan Adams and became a huge hit, the best-selling single of the year and stayed at No 1 for 16 weeks.

1992 Shakespeares Sister had their only No 1 UK single hit with **Stay** which stayed at the top for eight consecutive weeks.
The best-selling single of the year was Whitney Houston singing the song written by Dolly Parton, **I Will Always Love You.**

1993 **Pray** by Take That, written by Gary Barlow, was the first of twelve singles by the band to reach No 1 in the UK and the first of a run of four consecutive No 1's.

I'd Do Anything for Love (But I Won't Do That) was the song of the year and won Meat Loaf a Grammy Award for the Best Rock Solo Vocal Performance.

1994 The Most Beautiful Girl in the World by the unpronounceable Love Symbol, or 'The Artist Formerly Known as Prince' reached No 1.
The Manchester United football squad had the help of Status Quo, who wrote and sang along on their two week No 1 hit, **Come on You Reds.**

1995 - 1999

1995 Four artists had two No 1 hits this year. The Outhere Brothers with **Don't Stop (Wiggle Wiggle)** and **Boom Boom Boom**. Take That with **Back for Good** and **Never Forget** and Robson Green & Jerome Flynn with **Unchained Melody/ Bluebirds Over the White Cliffs of Dover** – the best seller of the year, and **I Believe/Up On the Roof.**

1996 This was a year with 23 No 1s. Most being at the top for only one week, but Fugees was No 1 twice with the same song **Killing Me Softly.** Firstly, for four weeks in June and then with a break for a week for **Three Lions (Football's Coming Home)** and another week in July.

1997 Elton John topped the charts for five weeks with **Candle in the Wind 1997**, a re-written and re-recorded version of **Candle in the Wind** as a tribute to the late Diana, Princess of Wales.
Another kind of tribute, this time to the popularity of the Teletubbies, their **Teletubbies say 'Eh-oh!'** stayed at No 1 for two weeks in December.

1998 The main soundtrack song from the blockbuster film Titanic provided Celine Dion with a hit, **My Heart Will Go On.**
Cher reinvented herself, and her song, **Believe** stayed at No 1 for seven weeks and was the year's best seller.

1999 Britney Spears made her debut single with **...Baby One More Time** which became a worldwide hit and sold over ten million copies.
Cliff Richard's **Millenium Prayer** is knocked off its 3 weeks at No 1 spot just in time for the boy band, Westlife, to make the Christmas No 1 with **I Have a Dream/Seasons in the Sun.**

IN THE 1990S

COOL BRITANNIA

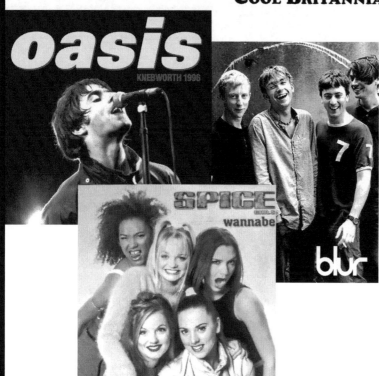

Throughout the mid and second half of the 1990s, Cool Britannia was a period of increased pride in the culture of the UK inspired by the 'Swinging London' of the 1960s pop culture. This brought about a huge success of 'Britpop' with groups such as Blur and Oasis and particularly, the Spice Girls.

Mel B, 'Scary Spice', Melanie C, 'Sporty Spice', Emma Bunton, 'Baby Spice', Geri Halliwell, 'Ginger Spice' and Victoria Beckham, 'Posh Spice' brought girl power to the fore. Their first single was 1996's iconic **Wannabe**, which established the group as a global phenomenon as 'Spice Mania' circled the globe. They scored the Christmas Number 1 single three years in a row and had nine UK No 1's in total.

LOVE IS ALL AROUND

In June 1994, Wet Wet Wet the Scottish soft rock band had a huge international hit, with 15 weeks as the UK No 1, with their cover of the 1960s hit by The Troggs, **Love Is All Around.** Their version was used on the soundtrack of the blockbuster film 'Four Weddings and a Funeral'.

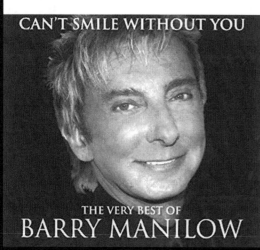

Richard Curtis, the director of the film, had approached Wet Wet Wet with a choice of three cover songs to record for the soundtrack, the other two being **I Will Survive** by Gloria Gaynor and Barry Manilow's **Can't Smile Without You**.

SCIENCE AND NATURE

THE HUBBLE TELESCOPE

The Hubble telescope is a general-purpose orbiting observatory. Orbiting approximately 380 mi (612 km) above Earth, the 12.5-ton Hubble Space Telescope has peered farther into the universe than any telescope before it. The Hubble, which was launched on April 24, 1990, has produced images with unprecedented resolution at visible, near-ultraviolet, and near-infrared wavelengths since its originally faulty optics were corrected in 1993.

Although ground-based telescopes are finally starting to catch up, the Hubble continues to produce a stream of unique observations. During the 1990s and now into the 2000s, the Hubble has revolutionised the science of astronomy, becoming one, if not the most, important instruments ever used in astronomy.

ADD TO BASKET

Mint Velvet Star Print Jumper, Pink

£69.00

Free Click & Collect over £30 & free returns
View delivery & returns options

Size: size guide

XS   S   M   L

XL

Add to your basket

♡ Add to wish list

ROYAL ALBERT OLD COUNTRY ROSES 40 PIECE DINNER TEA SET SERVICE TEASET ENGLAND

Condition: Used

Time left: 32m 7s (03 Mar, 2022 12:25:58 GMT)

Current bid: £185.00   [32 bids]

Bid amount   Submit bid

Enter £190.00 or more   ♡ Watch this item

Posts from United Kingdom

The first ever shopper bought online from Tesco in 1984 using her television remote control, but it was in 1990s, following the creation by Tim Berners-Lee of the World Wide Web server and browser and the commercialisation of the internet in 1991 giving birth to e-commerce, that online shopping really began to take off.

In 1995, Amazon began selling books online, computer companies started using the internet for *all* their transactions and Auction Web was set up by Pierre Omidyar as a site *"dedicated to bringing together buyers and sellers in an honest and open marketplace."* We now know this as eBay and we can buy just about anything on Amazon.

Comparison sites were set up in 1997 and in 1998, PayPal was founded, the way to pay online without having to share your financial information. By 1999, online only shops were beginning to emerge and paved the way for 'Click for Checkout' to become commonplace.

THE KYOTO PROTOCOL

In December 1997, at the instigation of the United Nations, representatives from 160 countries met in Kyoto, Japan, to discuss climate change and draft the Kyoto Protocol which aimed to restrict the greenhouse gas emissions associated with global warming.

The protocol focused on demands that 37 developed nations work to reduce their greenhouse gas emissions placing the burden on developed nations, viewing them as the primary sources and largely responsible for carbon emissions.

Developing nations were asked only to comply voluntarily, exempted from the protocol's requirements. The protocol's approach included establishing a 'carbon credits system' whereby nations can earn credits by participating in emission reduction projects in other nations. A carbon credit is a tradeable permit or certificate that provides the holder

SHOCK WAVES

A large earthquake, by British standards, occurred near Bishop's Castle, Shropshire on the Welsh Borders on 2 April 1990 at 13:46 GMT. With a magnitude of 5.1, the shock waves were felt over a wide area of Britain, from Ayrshire in the north to Cornwall in the south, Kent in the east and Dublin in the west.

Worldwide in 1990, there were 18 quakes of magnitude 7.0 or above and 134 quakes between 6.0 and 7.0, 4435 quakes between 4.0 and 5.0, 2755 quakes between 3.0 and 4.0, and 8618 quakes between 2.0 and 3.0. There were also 29800 quakes below magnitude 2.0 which people don't normally feel.

The strongest quake was north of Pulau Hulawa Island in Indonesia, registering 7.8 on the Richter scale.

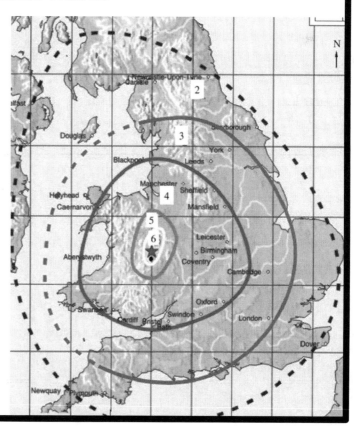

SPORT

1990 - 1994

1990 West Germany won the **FIFA World Cup** in Rome, defeating defending champions Argentina, 1–0 in the final.

The British golfer, Nick Faldo, had an amazing year, winning both the **Masters** and the Claret Jug at the **Open** at St Andrews, and capturing the PGA Player of the Year award, the first non-American to do so.

1991 At the **World Athletics** Championships in Tokyo, Mike Powell broke the 23 year-long world record **long jump** set by Bob Beamon, with a jump of 29' 4½".

1992 The rugby, **Five Nations Championship** is won by England who complete the Grand Slam for the second consecutive year.

The summer **Olympics** are held in Barcelona, Spain where Sally Gunnell takes home gold in the Women's 400 metres hurdles, Linford Christie triumphs in the Men's 100 metres, and rowers Matthew Pinsent and Steve Redgrave finish first in the Men's coxless pair, the first Olympic gold for all four athletes. In the **Paralympics**, Tanni Grey-Thompson in her debut Games, takes home four golds and a silver.

1993 Manchester United win the inaugural **English Premier League** title, their first league title in 26 years.

Shane Warne bowls the so-called 'Ball of the Century' in the first Test at Old Trafford. With his first ball against England, in his first **Ashes**, he bowled Mike Gatting out.

1994 Tiger Woods becomes the youngest man ever to win the **U.S. Amateur Golf Championships**, at age 18.

George Foreman becomes **Boxing's** oldest Heavyweight Champion at forty-five.

1995 - 1999

1995 In motor racing, Michael Schumacher wins his second consecutive **Drivers' Championship**, and Benetton wins its first and only Constructors' Championship.

British triple jumper Jonathan Edwards sets a world record in the **Athletics World Championships**, jumping 60' (18.29 m).

1996 The 95/96 **Rugby League** ends with Wigan declared champions.

Stephen Hendry wins the **World Snooker Championship** and remains the world number one.

1997 At 21, Tiger Woods becomes the youngest **Masters** winner in history, as well as the first non-white winner at Augusta. He set the scoring record at 270 and the record for the largest margin of victory at 12 strokes.

1998 In Japan, **Curling** is included in the Winter Olympics for the first time.

1999 Pete Sampras beats his biggest rival, Andre Agassi in the **Wimbledon Men's Singles** Final giving him his sixth win at the All England Club.

In the **US Open Tennis** final, at the age of 17, Serena Williams beats the number one player Martina Hingis and marks the beginning of one of the most dominant careers in the history of women's tennis.

IN THE 1990s

THE DANGEROUS SIDE TO SPORT

By 1993, Monica Seles, the Serbian-American tennis player, had won eight Grand Slam titles and was ranked No. 1 in the world. On April 30, 1993, then just 19, she was sitting on a courtside seat during a changeover in a match in Hamburg when a German man, said later to be a fan of the tennis star's German rival, Steffi Graf, leaned over a fence and stabbed her between the shoulder blades with a knife. The assailant was quickly apprehended and Seles was taken to the hospital with a wound half and inch deep in her upper back. She recovered from her physical injuries but was left with deep emotional scars and didn't play again professionally for another two years.

Leading up to the 1994 Winter Olympics, figure skater Nancy Kerrigan was attacked during a practice session. This had been 'commissioned' by the ex-husband of fellow skater, Tonya Harding and her bodyguard. Kerrigan was Harding's long-time rival and the one person in the way of her making the Olympic team, and she was desperate to win. Fortunately for Kerrigan, the injury left her with just bruises – no broken bones but she had to withdraw from the U.S. Figure Skating Championship the following night. However, she was still given a spot on the Olympic team and finished with a silver medal. Harding finished in eighth place and later had her U.S. Figure Skating Championship title revoked and was banned from the United States Figure Skating Association for life.

Also in 1994, Andrés Escobar the Colombian footballer, nicknamed 'The Gentleman' - known for his clean style of play and calmness on the pitch - was murdered following a second-round match against the US in the FIFA World Cup. This was reportedly in retaliation for Escobar having scored an own goal which contributed to the team's elimination from the tournament.

In 1997, Evander Holyfield and Mike Tyson's fight made headlines after Tyson was disqualified for biting off a part of his rival's ear, an infamous incident that would lead to the event being dubbed "The Bite Fight".

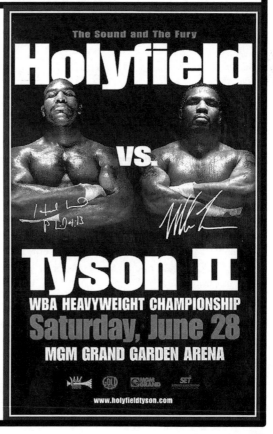

HAULAGE

The 1990s was a decade devoted to environmental considerations for haulage with top priority given to cleaner emissions and low noise levels. By the end of the decade, integrated IT solutions were being used to provide the tools necessary to increase efficiency and safety.

A significant factor in the 1990s was making the lorry more aerodynamic. A 20% saving in fuel consumption meant lower emissions and also the average transport operator could improve profits by up to 50%.

CRUISE SHIPS

The largest passenger ship of the 1990s was Royal Caribbean's 'Voyager of the Seas' at 137,276 gross tonnage and 310 m (1,020 ft) long.

This record was held between Oct 1999 and Sep 2000, when it was superseded by 'Explorer of the Seas', larger by only 12 GT. Royal Caribbean have, on order, and due 2024, an Oasis class cruiser of 231,000 gross tonnage, 362 m(1,188 ft) long.

THE HIGHWAY CODE

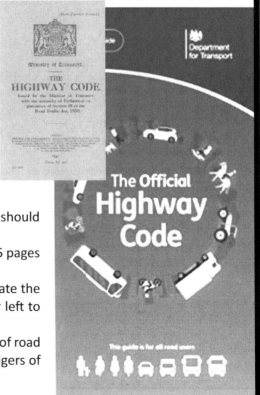

In July 1996 a separate written theory test was introduced to the Driving Test in the UK to replace questions asked about 'The Highway Code' whilst actually driving. Learner drivers were expected to know rather different information then from that published in the first edition of the Highway Code, price 1d, launched in 1931.

• In 1931 mirrors were not even mentioned.

• Drivers were advised to sound their horn when overtaking.

• At least 8 pages showed the various hand signals a driver should use. There was a single page in the current edition.

• Contained 18 pages (out of 24) of advice, compared to 135 pages in 2007.

• Included advice to drivers of horse drawn vehicles to 'rotate the whip above the head; then incline the whip to the right or left to show the direction in which the turn is to be made'.

It wasn't until the second edition of the Code that diagrams of road signs appeared, just 10 in all, plus a warning about the dangers of driving when tired or drinking and driving.

Renault Clio

Advertising for the first-generation Renault Clio introduced us to 'Nicole *et* Papa' and gave the small car a personality that appealed to drivers of all ages.

Ford Focus

The Focus replaced the previously very successful Escort. Ford wanted a 'World Car' to sell across all markets so the Focus was born and is still produced.

Toyota Previa

Toyota created the multi- purpose vehicle market with the Spacecruiser in the 80s, but the futuristic replacement, the Toyota Previa was a whole new approach to the people carrier.

Lexus LS 400

Toyota moved into the luxury market with the Lexus brand. The Lexus' flagship model is one of the most reliable vehicles ever built.

COCOTAXI

The auto-rickshaw began in Havana in the 1990s and soon spread to the whole of Cuba. These gas-scooters are named after their shape, that of a coconut and are made of a fibreglass shell with seats welded onto it. They can travel at about 30mph and because they are small, they weave and squeeze in and out of the city traffic. Blue Cocotaxis are for locals, yellow for tourists.

MOTORCYCLES

During the 1990s motorcycles started to evolve more quickly and there was a resurgence in the British biking industry with Triumph starting up production.

A bike lovers favourite however, was the 1995, Aprilia RS250.

NEW YEAR'S EVE 1999

THE MILLENNIUM BUG

Whilst the world was getting 'ready to party' there was an undercurrent of anxiety about the Y2K (year 2000) Bug and many people were scared. When complicated computer programmes were first written in the 1960s, programmers used a two-digit code for the year, leaving out the "19." As the year 2000 approached, many believed that the systems would not interpret the "00" correctly, making the year 2000 indistinguishable from 1900 causing a major malfunction.

It was particularly worrying to certain organisations. Banks calculate the rate for interest owed daily and instead of the rate for one day, if the 'clocks went back' their computers would calculate a rate of interest for **minus** 100 years!

Airlines felt they were at a very great risk. All scheduled flights are recorded on computers and liable to be affected and, if the computer reverted to 1900, well, there were very few airline flights that year!
Power plants were threatened, depending on routine computer maintenance for safety checks, such as water pressure or radiation levels, the wrong date would wreck the calculations and possibly put nearby residents at risk.

Huge sums were spent to prepare for the consequences and both software and hardware companies raced to fix it by developing "Y2K compliant" programmes. Midnight passed on the 1 January 2000 and the crisis failed to materialise - planes did not fall from the sky, power stations did not melt down and thousands of people who had stocked up on food, water, even arms, or purchased backup generators or withdrawn large sums of money in anticipation of a computer-induced apocalypse, could breathe easily again.

The Millennium Dome

Officially called the O2, the huge construction and tourist attraction alongside the Thames in Greenwich, London was initially built to house an exhibition for the approach of the 21st Century. Designed by Sir Richard Rogers, the central dome is the largest in the world. On December 31, 1999, a New Year's Eve celebration at the dome was attended by some 10,500 people, including the Prime Minister, Tony Blair, and the Queen. Opening the next day, the Millennium Dome exhibition lasted until December 31, 2000.

AND A NEW MILLENNIUM

MEMORABILIA AND MONUMENTS

The Millennium Wheel Better known as the London Eye, at 135m (443 ft) it is Europe's tallest cantilevered observation wheel. Situated on the South Bank of the Thames when opened it used to offer the highest public viewing point in London until superseded in 2013 by the 245m high (804 ft) observation deck on the 72nd floor of The Shard.

Portsmouth's Millennium Tower opened five years late and officials were so concerned that people may actually have forgotten what the millennium was, that they gave it a new name, **The Spinnaker Tower**.

The Millennium Bridge is a steel suspension bridge for pedestrians over the River Thames linking Bankside with the City of London. Londoners nicknamed it the "Wobbly Bridge" after pedestrians experienced an alarming swaying motion on its opening day.

Lots of memorabilia was produced to mark the new millennium. Some pieces are timeless classics and others will soon be forgotten.

KEY EVENTS 2000-2009

2000:
Jan: Celebrations take place throughout the UK on the 1st and the Millennium Dome is officially opened by The Queen.

Aug 4th: Queen Elizabeth the Queen Mother celebrates her hundredth birthday

2001:
Feb: The Foot and Mouth disease crisis begins. Over 6 million cows and sheep are killed to halt the disease.

Jun: Labour wins the General Election. David Cameron is a new entrant, Edward Heath retires, and William Hague resigns as leader of the Conservatives.

2002:
Jan: The Euro is officially introduced in the Eurozone countries.

Jun: The Golden Jubilee. A special service is held in St Paul's Cathedral to mark the Queen's 50 years on the throne. Celebrations take place all over the country.

2003:
Mar: The United States, along with coalition forces primarily from the United Kingdom, initiates war on Iraq

May: BBC Radio 4 airs a report stating that the government claimed in its dossier, that Iraq could deploy weapons of mass destruction within forty-five minutes knowing the claim to be dubious.
Jul: Dr David Kelly, the weapons expert who was the reporter's source, is found dead.

2004:
Jan: The Hutton Inquiry into the circumstances of the death of Dr Kelly is published. The UK media, in general, condemns the report as a whitewash.

Jul: A new Countryside Code is published in advance of the 'Right to Roam' coming into effect in September across England and Wales.

TERRORISM

2001: On the 11th September, Al-Qaeda terrorists hijack civilian airliners and fly two into the Twin Towers of the World Trade Centre in New York, which collapse. There are 3,000 fatalities including 67 British nationals.

SOCIAL MEDIA

2004: In February, Mark Zuckerberg launches 'The Facebook', later renamed 'Facebook' as an online social networking website for Harvard University Students. In 2006 it was opened up to anyone over the age of 13.

EXPLOSION

2005: On the morning of 11 December, the UK experienced its largest explosion since World War Two. A huge blast at the Buncefield fuel depot in Hemel Hempstead, was heard as far away as the Netherlands and caused the UK's biggest blaze in peacetime which shrouded much of south-east England in smoke.

HIGH SPEED TRAINS

2007: In November, the Queen officially opened 'High Speed 1' and 'St Pancras International' station. The Channel Tunnel first opened to Eurostar in 1994, with trains running from Waterloo, but the new 69-mile link meant the journey from London to Paris reduced to 2 hrs 15 minutes and to Brussels 1 hr 51 min.

2005:
Apr: Prince Charles marries Camilla Parker Bowles at a private ceremony at Windsor Guildhall.

Aug: Hurricane Katrina devastates much of the U.S. Gulf Coast from Louisiana to the Florida Panhandle killing an estimated 1,836 people

2006:
Jul: Twitter is launched, becoming one of the largest social media platforms in the world.

Nov: Alexander Litvinenko a British-naturalised Russian defector dies of polonium poisoning in London.

2007:
Jun: Tony Blair resigns as Prime Minister and Gordon Brown is elected unopposed.

Jul: England introduces a ban on smoking in enclosed public places in line with Scotland, Wales and N. Ireland.

2008:
Mar: Terminal 5 is opened at London Heathrow but IT problems cause over 500 flights to be cancelled

Nov: St Hilda's College admits male undergraduates and ceases to be the last single-sex college at Oxford.

Dec: Woolworths shuts down in the UK.

2009:
Jul: The largest haul of Anglo-Saxon treasure ever found, the Staffordshire Hoard, is first uncovered buried beneath a field near Litchfield. 4,600 items amounting to 11 lb of gold, 3lb of silver and 3.5k pieces of garnet cloisonné jewellery.

Oct: The independent audit of MPs expenses is completed and exposes a widespread parliamentary scandal.

2010:

Jan: In the Chilcott Inquiry, set up in 2009, Tony Blair is questioned in public for the first time about his decision to take the UK to war against Iraq.

May: The General Election results in a Hung Parliament. An alliance is formed between the Tories and the Liberal Democrats.

2011:

Feb: An earthquake of 6.3 magnitude devastates Christchurch, New Zealand. Hundreds of people are killed.

Apr: Prince William marries Catherine Middleton in Westminster Abbey.

2012:

Jun: The UK begins celebrations of the Queen's Diamond Jubilee. Events include a pageant on the Thames and a Pop Concert outside Buckingham Palace

Jul: The summer Olympic Games are held in London, making it the first city to host them for a third time.

2013:

Jul: A new Marriage Act receives Royal Assent and same-sex marriage becomes legal in England and Wales.

Aug: A burger, grown from bovine stem cells in a laboratory, is cooked and eaten in London. The same month, a 15 ton 'fatburg' is removed after completely blocking a London sewer.

2014:

Mar: Prince Harry launches the Invictus Games for wounded soldiers.

Mar: The first gay weddings take place in England and Wales.

THE SHARD

2012: In July, The Shard, an iconic 'vertical city' is officially opened in London. It is the tallest building in Europe and the tallest habitable free-standing structure in the UK at 1,016ft (309.6 m)

THE ARAB SPRING

2010: 'The Arab Spring', a series of anti-government protests, uprisings, and armed rebellions spread across much of the Arab world. Starting in Tunisia it spread to Libya, Egypt, Yemen, Syria and Bahrain. Amongst leaders to be deposed was Gaddafi of Libya.

BREXIT

June 2016: After months of heated, angry argument and debate, the referendum on whether to leave the EU or remain within it, is held. Nearly 30m people take part and the result is to leave the EU: 51.9% votes to 48.1%.

March 2017: Article 50 is invoked and the two-year countdown to departure begins.
March 2019: Parliament rejected Theresa May's EU withdrawal agreement and a new deadline is set by The European Council to leave, with or without an Agreement, at the end of Oct 2019.
Jun 2019: Unable to 'deliver Brexit', Theresa May steps down and in Jul 2019: Boris Johnson becomes Prime Minister.
Oct 2019: The deadline to leave passes, and the EU agrees to a new date, end of Jan 2020. Commemorative Brexit coins are melted down.
Jan 2020: Johnson signs the Withdrawal Agreement.

January 31st 2020: At 11pm, the UK leaves the European Union and marks the moment with a party in Parliament Square.

2015:
Jan: Two Al-Qaeda gunmen kill 12 and injure 11 more at the Paris headquarters of the satirical newspaper Charlie Hebdo.

May: The General Election is won by David Cameron for the Conservatives with an outright majority of 331 seats.
Jun: The 800th anniversary of the Magna Carta.

2016:
Jun: The UK Referendum to leave the EU, Brexit, takes place and the majority vote is 'Yes'. David Cameron later resigns.
Jul: On July 14, Bastille Day (Independence Day), a terrorist drives a truck through a crowded promenade in Nice, France. 87 people are killed.
Nov: Donald Trump becomes US President.

2017:
There are a string of deadly terror attacks in Britain including : Westminster Bridge, the Manchester Arena and London Bridge.
Jun: The Tories lose their majority in Theresa May's general election gamble.

2018:
Apr: The UK, France, and United States order the bombing of Syrian military bases.

May: Prince Harry marries the American actress Meghan Markle in St George's Chapel, Windsor Castle. It is thought 1.9m people watched on TV worldwide.

2019:
Jun: Theresa May resigns as Prime Minister. Before she goes, she agrees a new legally binding target to reach net zero by 2050.
Jul: Boris Johnson becomes Prime Minister.

"One Ring to Rule Them All'

Based on the fantasy, adventure epics written by JRR Tolkein in the 1930s and 40s, Peter Jackson's trilogy of films became a major financial success, received widespread acclaim and is ranked among the greatest film trilogies ever made. The three films were shot simultaneously in Jackson's native New Zealand between 1999 and 2000 and with a budget of $281m, was one of the most ambitious film projects ever undertaken.

The **Lord of the Rings: The Fellowship of the Ring** was nominated for 13 Oscars and won four, one of which, unsurprisingly, was for the Special Effects as did **The Lord of the Rings: The Two Towers** and **The Lord of the Rings: The Return of the King**.

Peter Jackson then went on to make a further three films based on Tolkein's Middle Earth saga, **'The Hobbit: An Unexpected Journey**, **The Hobbit: The Desolation of Smaug** and **The Hobbit: The Battle of the Five Armies**. The three films were prequels to the Lord of the Rings saga and together, the six films became one of the 'greatest movie series franchise' of all time.

'The Greatest Fairy Tale Never Told'

In 2002, the Oscar for Best Animated Feature was awarded for the first time to **Shrek**, the large, surly, sarcastic, wisecracking, Scottish-accented greenish ogre with a round face and stinky breath who took a mud shower outdoors near his home in the swamp and blew fart bubbles in a mud pool! But being a goodhearted ogre, children and adults alike, loved him!

'A Film of Our Times'

The Social Network made in 2010, is an American biographical drama portraying the founding of the social networking phenomenon Facebook and the resulting lawsuits. Based on the book, 'The Accidental Billionnaires' by

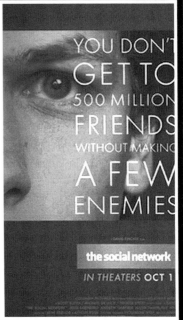

Ben Mezrich the film was nominated for the Oscars in 2011 winning The Best Adapted Screenplay but missing out on Best Picture to **The King's Speech**.

In The 21st Century

'Precious Pieces'

In 2007 Damien Hirst wowed the art-world with his fabulous **For the Love of God** a life-size platinum cast of an eighteenth century human skull, covered by 8,601 flawless diamonds, inset with the original skull's teeth. At the front of the cranium is a 52.4 carat pink

diamond. The work is reputed to be the most expensive contemporary artwork ever made and was *allegedly* entitled **For the Love of God** in response to a question posed by the artist's mother "For the love of God, what are you going to do next?"! It has become one of the most widely recognised works of contemporary art and represents the artist's continued interest in mortality and the fragility of life.

Screaming Success

In May, 2012, a pastel version of **The Scream**, by Norwegian painter Edvard Munch, sells for $120m in New York City, setting a new world record for a work of art at auction.

'Question Everything, Believe Nothing'

Conspiracy theory is not a new phenomenon but in 2001, Dan Brown introduced the world to Robert Langdon and a whole new collection of conspiracies and secret societies, with his first book, **Angels & Demons**. Set in the Vatican and Rome, Langdon must decipher a labyrinthine trail of ancient symbols if he is to defeat the Illuminati, a monstrous secret brotherhood.

When **The Da Vinci Code** came along in 2003, hordes of tourists descended on Paris, staring at the Mona Lisa as though she held the secret to life and traipsing around cathedrals and monuments, speculating on the Holy Grail and obsessed with the Priory of Sion and Opus Dei.

By 2009 in **The Lost Symbol**, Brown had set his sights on the Capitol Building, Washington DC and the shadowy, mythical world in which the Masonic secrets abound.

Back in Italy in 2013, this time Florence, for **Inferno**, Langdon is also back to hidden passageways and ancient secrets that lie behind historic facades, deciphering a sequence of codes buried deep within Renaissance artworks with only the help of a few lines from Dante's Inferno.

The Top Ten UK Singles of the 21ˢᵗ Century

YEAR

2013   **Happy** by Pharrell Williams.

2002   Will Young's **Anything is Possible**

2013   **Blurred Lines** sung by Robin Thicke featuring TI and Pharrell Williams.

2014   Mark Ronson and featuring Bruno Mars with **Uptown Funk**

2011   Adele singing **Someone Like You**

2011   **Moves Like Jagger** by Maroon 5 featuring Christina Aguilera

2012   Gotye featuring Kimbra and **Somebody That I Used to Know**

2013   **Wake Me Up** by Avicii

2009   The Black Eyed Peas with **I Gotta Feeling**

2013   Daft Punk featuring Pharrell Williams and **Get Lucky**

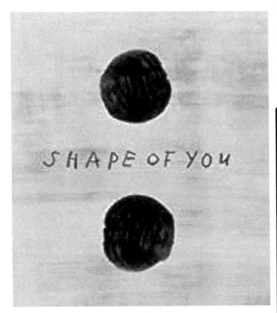

Since 2014 streaming has counted towards sales, called "combined sales", at the rate of 100 streams equal to one download or physical purchase, although the singles chart no longer uses this ratio. The biggest selling song of the 21ˢᵗ Century, based on combined physical, download and streaming sales, *and as of Sep 2017*, is **The Shape of You** by Ed Sheeran, (2017) with sales of just over 3 million.

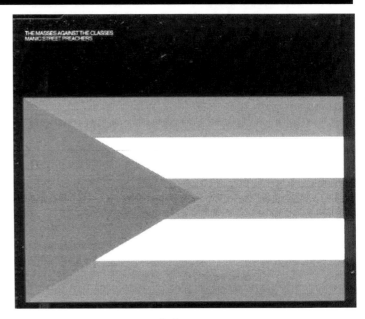

First of the Century

The first No 1 Single of the 21ˢᵗ Century in the UK Charts is **Manic Street Preachers** with The Masses Against the Classes. This song by Welsh rock band was released as a limited-edition single being deleted, removed from wholesale supply, on the day of release. Despite this, it peaked at No 1.

Millennial Music

What about the music the Millennials, born in the 80s and 90s, like to listen to? It may eventually fit just as well onto a "best songs of all time" playlist alongside the likes of The Beatles and The Supremes. These are some of the 21st-century pop songs that could stand the test of time and they are all female artists too!

Single Ladies (Put a Ring on It) by Beyoncé. **Umbrella** by Rihanna featuring Jay-Z. **Shake it Off** by Taylor Swift. **Toxic** by Britney Spears. **Rolling in the Deep** by Adele and **Firework** by Katy Perry.

However, those of us **Born in 1962** are not surprised to know, that in 2019, a US study found that golden oldies stick in millennials' minds far more than the relatively bland, homogeneous pop of today. A golden age of popular music lasted from the 1960s to the 1990s, academics claimed. Songs from this era proved to be much more memorable than tunes released in the 21st century.

FASHION

Music and fashion have been intertwined since the 1960s and nothing appears to be changing at the beginning of the 21st Century. The young will imitate their idols. Today though, designers are taking their inspiration from the past and bringing it back into the future, the new millennium fashion is a 'fusion' of the 60's, 70's and 80's, feeding our freedom to 'wear what we want, whenever we want'.

However, one major shift of emphasis will be the consumer's demand for environmental sustainability and social responsibility and to move away from 'fast, disposable fashion'. Fashion began moving at breakneck speeds in the 1960's, and the young wanted cheaply made clothing to follow these new trends. Fashion brands had to find ways to keep up with the ever-increasing demand for affordable clothing and this led to the massive growth in manufacturing being outsourced to the developing world, saving us millions of pounds in labour costs.

In the 21st Century we are aware of dreadful labour practices and the enormous amounts of waste. The industry will need to slow down for the customer mindful of how their clothes are made.

SCIENCE & TECHNOLOGY

Watch everywhere.

Stream unlimited movies and TV shows on your phone, tablet, laptop, and TV without paying more.

The technological innovations of the first two decades of the 21st century have drastically revolutionised people's day-to-day lives. Television, radio, paperback novels, cinemas, landline telephones and even letter writing can be, and have been by millions, replaced by connected devices, digital books, Netflix, and communications using apps such as Twitter, Facebook or Snapchat. We have marvels such as personalized hover boards, self-driving cars and, of course, the smartphone. All commonplace now when just a decade and a half ago most were unfathomable.

Consumers watch films, listen to music, record the day, book holidays and carry out their shopping with a few taps on a screen and even people who have never owned a computer are digitally connected 24-hours a day via their smartphones.

E-readers and Kindle

E-readers have been under development since the 1940s, but it was not until 2004 when Sony first brought out an e-reader, and then, when demand for e-books increased, Kindle arrived in 2007, that they became mainstream. An eBook is a text-based publication in digital form stored as electronic files. E-readers are small, convenient, light and have a huge storage capacity that allows for reading whilst

travelling, making electronic notes and character summaries and more. Pages do not exist in eBooks and where the reader is 'up to' is altered depending on what font size and layout the reader has chosen, which means 'your place' is displayed as a percentage of the whole text.

Although it was feared e-readers were the death knell for the traditional book, it appears not to be the case as it seems many people really do like to hold a physical book in their hands, feeling the weight. After all, even Kindle uses a **'bookmark'** to hold our place!

3D Printing

The 3D printer has been around since the 1980s. Now, the know-how is getting used for everything from automobile components to bridges to much less painful ballet slippers, synthetic organs, custom dental work, prosthetic limbs, and custom hearing aids.

IN THE 21ST CENTURY

The Future of Transport

Driverless Cars
Self-driving cars are expected to be on the roads more quickly, and in greater numbers, than was anticipated.

Floating Trains
There are already Maglev – magnetic levitation – trains in use. The Shanghai Maglev connects their Airport with a station on the outskirts of the city. At speeds up to 268 mph.

Hyperloop
High speed bullet trains or transport capsules are being developed to provide unprecedented speeds of 600mph.

Solar Panel Roads
Which also generate electricity are being tested in, amongst other countries, France, the US and China as well as on bike lanes in the Netherlands.

Touch Screens

Smartphones, tablets, and even Smartwatches all need one underlying technology without which they cannot succeed. The touch screen, as we know it integrated into consumer products, took off in the 2000s and is now everywhere, homes, cars, restaurants, shops, planes, wherever. Unlike other computer devices, touchscreens are unique because they allow the user to interact directly with what's on the screen, unlike a mouse that moves a cursor.

In 2007, the original iPhone was released and revolutionised the phone industry, its touchscreen can change between a dialling pad, a keyboard, a video, a game, or a myriad of other apps. The Apple iPad was released in 2010 and with it, a wave of tablets from competitors. Not only are most of our phones equipped with touchscreens, but portable computers are too.

2000 Tiger Woods wins the **US Open** golf by 15 shots, a record for all majors.

Australia wins the **Rugby League World Cup** against New Zealand. Italy joins the Five Nations **Rugby Union** making it the Six Nations.

2001 Sir Donald Bradman dies. He retains the highest **Test Match** batting average of 99.94.

Venus Williams wins the **Ladies Singles Final at Wimbledon**.

2002 "Lewis–Tyson: Is On". Lennox won the fight by a knockout to retain the **WBC Heavyweight Boxing** Crown.

Arsenal matched Man chester United with their third Double, **FA Cup** and **League title**.

2003 Mike Wier becomes the first Canadian and the first *left-handed golfer* to win the **Masters**.

Serena Williams beats her sister Venus in the **Ladies Singles Final at Wimbledon**.

2004 In Athens, Kelly Holmes wins **Olympic Gold** for the 800 & 1500m. Britain also win Gold in the 4x100m relay. Michael Schumacher, in his Ferrari, wins a record 12 of the first 13 races of the season, and wins the **F1** World Drivers Championship.

2005 Ellen MacArthur attains the World Record for **Sailing** the fastest solo circumnavigation of the globe. In **Cricket**, England win The Ashes.

2006 Justin Gatlin equals Powell's **100m world record** time of 9.77 seconds in Quatar.

In golf, Europe wins the **Ryder Cup** for the third straight time, defeating the USA 18½–9½.

2007 27 January – After nearly 50 years, the final edition of **'Grandstand'**, the BBC flagship sports programme is aired.

Australia completes a 5–0 whitewash over England in the **Ashes Series**, the first time since 1920–21 that one team has won all the Tests in the series.

2008 At the Beijing Olympics, Team GB dominate the **Cycling**, winning 14 medals, including 8 Gold.

Usain Bolt thundered to victory in the **100m Olympic final** at the Bird's Nest in a world record time. He also broke the world record in the 200m.

2009 Jenson Button and Brawn GP secure their first and only **F1 Drivers' Championship** and Constructors' Championship titles, respectively.

In an incident that shocked the entire sporting world, the **Sri Lankan cricket team** was attacked by terrorists while heading to the stadium to play a match.

2010 At his debut in the US, Amir Khan, the British boxer retains his **WBA Light Welterweight** title for the second time.
Alberto Contador of Spain, wins his 3rd **Tour de France** and 5th Grand Tour.

2011 Rory McIlroy fired a 69 in the final round of the **US Open**, breaking the record with a 268 and winning by eight strokes. He becomes the youngest US Open winner since Bobby Jones in 1923.

2012 At the **London Olympics** on 'Super Saturday', Jessica Ennis-Hill, Greg Rutherford and Mo Farah all win gold in an unforgettable 44 minutes inside the Olympic Stadium. On this one single day twelve British athletes win gold medals across six events

Bradley Wiggins wins the **Tour de France**, the first British rider ever to do so and Mark Cavendish wins the final stage on the Champs-Élysées for a record fourth successive year.

2013 The **Boston Marathon** is bombed by terrorists. At **Wimbldon**, Andy Murray defeats Novak Djokovic to become the first British winner of the **Men's Singles** since Fred Perry in 1936. He earns his second Grand Slam title

2014 The first ever Invictus Games is hosted in London with over 400 competitors from 13 nations. The FA Cup Final is won by Arsenal, a joint record 11th Cup having beaten Hull City 4-3 after extra time.

2015 In Golf, Jordan Spieth led from the start in the **Masters**, shooting a record-tying 270, 18 under, to win his first major at the age of 21. Later in the year he also wins the U.S. Open.
The **Grand National** at Aintree is won by 'Many Clouds' ridden by Leighton Aspell, his second consecutive Grand National Victory.

2016 Leicester City, 5,000-1 outsiders for the title, win the **Premier League.**
Former Leicester City player Gary Lineker stated that if Leicester won the league, he would present Match of the Day in his underwear!

2017 Roger Federer becomes the undisputed **King of Wimbledon** with his record 8th win.
Chris Froome wins his 4th **Tour de France**.
In the **Women's World Cup Cricket**, England beat India by nine runs in the final at Lords.

2018 The **Tour de France** general classification was won by Geraint Thomas of Team Sky, his first win.
Roger Bannister, the first man to run a four-minute mile died this year.

2019 At the **Cheltenham Festival**, 'Frodon' ridden by Bryony Frost wins the Ryanair Chase. She is the first woman to ride a Grade One winner at Cheltenham.
Tiger Woods wins his first major in 11 years at the **Masters**.

2020 At the Tokyo Olympics, Lamont Jacobs wins the **100m** sprint and is the new 'World's Fastest Man'.

1947: Britain was struck this year by 'the perfect storm'. Record snowfall followed by a sudden thaw which culminated in heavy rain produced what is widely considered to be Britain's worst flood. Over 100,000 homes were directly affected and over 750,000 hectares of farmland submerged. The damages at the time totalled around £12 million, £300 million in today's terms.

1952: In August, the tiny village of Lynmouth, north Devon, suffered the worst river flood in English history. On the 15th, just over 9in (230mm) of rain fell over north Devon and west Somerset. The East and West Lyn rivers flooded and tons of water, soil, boulders and vegetation descended over Exmoor to meet at sea level in Lynmouth. The village was destroyed. The West Lyn rose 60 ft (18.25 m) above the normal level at its highest point and 34 people lost their lives.

1953: The great North Sea flood of January caused catastrophic damage and loss of life in Scotland, England, Belgium and The Netherlands and was Britain's worst peacetime disaster on record claiming the lives of 307 people. There were no severe flood warnings in place and the combination of gale-force winds, low pressure and high tides brought havoc to over 1,000 miles of coastline and 32,000 people were displaced because of flooding.

1963: Britain had the coldest winter in living memory, lasting for three long months from Dec 1962. The 6th March 1963 was the first morning of the year without frost anywhere in Britain.

It was so cold that rivers, lakes and even the sea froze over. On 25 February a record low of -22c in Braemar was recorded and 95,000 miles of road were snowbound.

1987: The Hurricane that wasn't supposed to be! Weatherman Michael Fish, like other forecasters, didn't see it coming. Eighteen people died and over 15 million trees were lost when in October, the hurricane-force winds blasted through south-east England. Meteorological research revealed a completely new weather phenomenon called the 'sting jet', a 100mph wind, the first to be documented in Britain.

WEATHER

2003: In August a new UK record was set for the 'Hottest Day in History' when temperatures reached 38.5c (101.3f) in Faversham, Kent. By the end of the summer, the heat had claimed the lives of over 2,000 people in Britain, mostly through heat stroke or dehydration.

An almost empty reservoir

1976: Britain had its hottest three months in living memory and it should have been the perfect summer, but with the continued sunshine came the worst drought in 150 years. Rivers dried up, soil began to crack and water supplies were on the verge of running out in Britain's most dramatic heatwave of the 20th Century. The drought was so rare, Britain appointed its first ever minister for drought, Denis Howell. He was nicknamed the minister for rain as the day after they installed him the heavens opened for the next two months!

2000: Following a wet spring and early summer, the autumn was the wettest on record for over 270 years. Repeated heavy rainfall in October and November caused significant and extensive flooding, inundated 10,000 homes and businesses. Train services cancelled, major motorways closed, and power supplies disrupted.

2007: Summer 2007 was the wettest on record with 414.1mm of rain falling across England and Wales in May, June and July - more than at any time since records began in 1766.
Although the rain was exceptionally heavy, climatologists say it was not the result of global warming. A report by the Centre for Ecology and Hydrology concluded the rain was a freak event, not part of any historical trend.

2004: A flash flood submerged the Cornish village of Boscastle during the busy holiday period when over 60 mm of rain (typically a month's rainfall) fell in two hours. The ground was already saturated due to two weeks of above average rainfall and the Jordan and Valency rivers burst their banks causing about two billion litres of water to rush down the valley straight into Boscastle. This led to the flash flood which caused total devastation to the area, but miraculously, no loss of life.

GLOBAL DISASTERS OF

AUSTRALIAN BUSH FIRES

Australia experienced the worst bushfire season ever in 2019-2020 with fires blazing for months in large parts of the country. Around 126,000 square kilometres of land and thousands of buildings were destroyed and at least 33 people died. Victoria and New South Wales were the worst affected and a state of emergency was declared in the capital city, Canberra.

Australia is used to bushfires, they are a natural part of the country's summer and native trees like eucalyptus need the heat for their seeds to be released, but this season they started earlier than usual, spread much faster, burned hotter and lasted longer, from June 2019 until March 2020, with the worst of the fires happening in December and January.

2019 was Australia's hottest and driest year on record with temperatures hitting 40c and above in every state and these hot, dry and windy conditions made the fires bigger and more intense than normal.

THE INDIAN OCEAN TSUNAMI

In the early morning of December 26, 2004, there was a massive and sudden movement of the Earth's crust under the Indian Ocean. This earthquake was recorded at magnitude 9 on the Richter Scale and as it happened under the ocean, the sea floor was pushed upwards, by as much as 40m, displacing a huge volume of water and causing the devastating tsunami which hit the shores of Indonesia, Sri Lanka, India, Thailand, and the Maldives.

Within 20 minutes the waves, reaching 30 feet high, and racing at the speed of a jet aircraft, engulfed the shoreline of Banda Aceh on the northern tip of Sumatra, killing more than 100,000 people and pounding the city into rubble. Then, moving on to Thailand, India and Sri Lanka, an estimated total of 250,000 people were killed, including many tourists on the beaches of Thailand. Millions more people were displaced, and eight hours later, and 5,000 miles from its Asian epicentre, the tsunami claimed its final casualties on the coast of South Africa.

THE 21ST CENTURY

HURRICANE KATRINA

Hurricane Katrina hit the coast of Louisiana on 29th August 2005. A Category 3 storm, it caused destruction from central Florida to Texas, but most lives were lost, and damage caused in New Orleans. It passed over Miami where the 80mph winds uprooted trees and killed two people. Hurricanes need warm ocean water to keep up speed and strength, so Katrina weakened whilst over the land to a tropical storm. Crossing back into the Gulf of Mexico, it quickly regained hurricane status and at its largest, was so wide, its diameter stretched

right across the Gulf. Katrina crossed back over the coast near Biloxi, Mississippi, where winds were the strongest and damage was extensive. However, later that morning, the first of 50 old levees broke in New Orleans, and a surge of floodwater poured into the low-lying city.

COVID 19 A GLOBAL PANDEMIC

The first human cases of COVID-19, the coronavirus disease caused by SARS CoV-2, were first reported from Wuhan City, China, in December 2019. Environmental samples taken in a food market in Wuhan where wild and farmed animals were traded, were positive for the virus and it is still unconfirmed whether the market was the origin of the virus or was just the setting for its initial spread.

The virus spread rapidly throughout China and has been found in 202 other countries, reaching Britain, from Europe, in late January 2020 and in March, the 'Stay at Home Order' or lockdown, was introduced. Non-essential travel was banned, schools were shut along with many businesses and venues. We were told to stay 6ft apart from others, self-isolate and, if at risk, to shield.

SEX AND SEXISM SELLS

Attitudes towards many aspects of our lives have changed significantly since the 1970s. One very entertaining way to see some of these changes is to look at the advertisements of the times.

Smirnoff made fun of the feminism movement in the 1970s.

TOWARDS WOMEN

Kleenex for Men Tissues aren't only for men.
Kleenex for Men aren't only for colds. They're quite simply the best tissues you can buy . . . big and strong and soft.
Anything other tissues can do, they can do better. So next time you need a tissue, be bold.
Use his.

use 'his' Kleenex
TISSUES

*Regd. trade mark Kimberly-Clark Corp.

Your glow... his delight

No skin glows like beautiful, smooth black skin and that's one of the things about you that delights him so. But dark blotches, rough patches, bumps and blackheads can turn off that glow and turn him off, too.
So if you have a skin problem, don't despair. Bleach & Glow Cream gives you a one-step beauty treatment. One cream. One step. Once a day.
When you smooth on Bleach & Glow, it soon vanishes while its special medication actually works deep beneath the skin. In just a few weeks your skin looks clearer, smoother, finer. You are one soft, glowing even tone all over.
Now you know how to keep your glow his delight. One cream. One step. Once a day—Bleach & Glow Cream—in jar or tube.

BLEACH & GLOW
a new life for your skin and you

1971: Change was about to happen, 'Because I'm Worth It' reflected women's rights, encouraging women to embrace their ambitions fearlessly and believe in their self-worth every day.

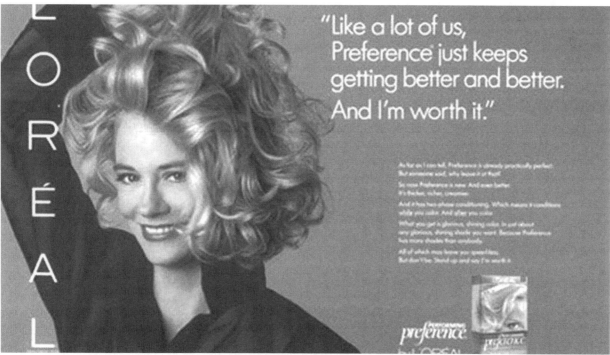

"Like a lot of us, Preference just keeps getting better and better. And I'm worth it."

We've come a long way from saying women are inferior to men, but there can still be subtle sexism in adverts today however, research is showing that when people are portrayed in general, not just men or women, in non-stereotypical ways the ads perform better.

109

SIZE MATTERS

In Great Britain, cars were smaller in the 70s than they are now. A four-seater, just big enough for you, the family and a couple of suitcases was the norm, you didn't have to squeeze into parking spaces and there was no need to dread driving down country lanes. By the 21st Century, cars have become bigger and the ubiquitous SUV is everywhere. Even the not-so Mini Cooper has evolved since lorry drivers struggled to see the car in their side view mirrors and is now 61% bigger than the original.

The major reasons for the increase in size are firstly, they are produced abroad and therefore not designed with the British roads in mind; safety considerations such as airbags and crumple zones need more room to accommodate; manufacturers can charge more for a larger car whilst the cost of producing it is not much more than producing a small car and finance deals have removed the necessity of finding the cash up front and enable the purchase of bigger, luxury, models.

THE MINI THEN
Length 120ins Width 50ins Weight 580Kg

THE MINI NOW
Length 150ins Width 68ins Weight 1150Kg

THE FORD FIESTA THEN
Length 140ins Width 62ins Weight 750Kg

THE FORD FIESTA NOW
Length 160ins Width 69ins Weight 1200Kg

In just 50 years cars have become longer, wider and much heavier. The Mini has doubled in weight, the Fiesta is 60% heavier and SUV versions of a car are wider and heavier than their saloon counterparts. SUVs are very popular but use more fuel and have more emissions than the non SUV versions.

SUV electric cars use more electricity than non SUVs, and are more expensive to buy.

TOWARDS CARS

THE BMW 3 SERIES THEN
Length 171ins Width 63ins Weight 1100Kg

THE BMW 3 SERIES SUV
Length 185ins Width 74ins Weight 1885Kg

THE ROLLS ROYCE CULLIAN
Length 210ins Width 80ins Weight 2739Kg

HOW IN CAR TECHNOLOGY HAS CHANGED

The 70s introduced the in-car cassette tape player

The 80s brought the CD-Radio player

The 90s brought in car telephones

The 2020s brought in self driving cars

And the future? Manufacturers are already working on making displays that respond to gestures, no touch screens necessary; you will be able to start your car or open the boot with your fingerprint and all the information you might need will be displayed on 'smart glass' in your windscreen!

HOW ATTITUDES HAVE CHANGED

It is a truth now universally acknowledged that smoking is bad for your health, but it wasn't always so. Cigarettes had been promoted as 'healthy', socially improving and fun! Some brands kept customer loyalty by offering gift vouchers.

As early as 1950 a report in the British Medical Journal had suggested a link between smoking and lung cancer and by 1962 the Royal College of Physicians had enough evidence to push for a ban on advertising.

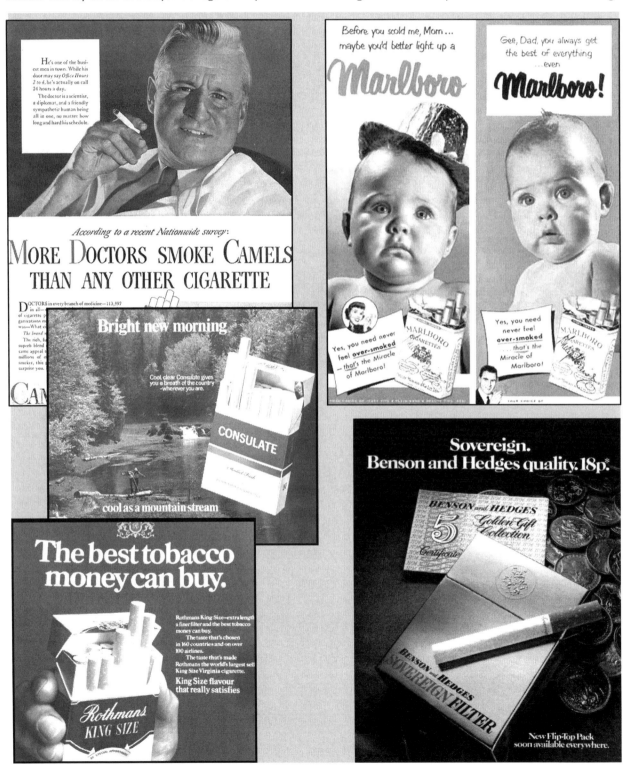

TOWARDS SMOKING

TIME LINE OF LAW CHANGES

1965: Television Commercials Banned

1971: All cigarette packets required a warning stating "WARNING by H.M. Government, SMOKING CAN DAMAGE YOUR HEALTH".

1982: The British Medical Association requested a ban on all forms of tobacco advertising.

1986: In 1986 adverts were banned in cinemas and it wasn't permitted to show a person smoking in an ad for any product or service.

1987: Smoking and cigarette advertising is banned on the underground – but more for safety reasons than those of health.

1991: The EU stated that all cigarettes must have two warnings on the packet, one on the front stating 'TOBACCO SERIOUSLY DAMAGES HEALTH' and another warning on the back such as "Smoking clogs the arteries and causes heart attacks and strokes".

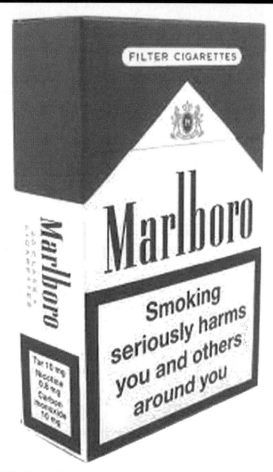

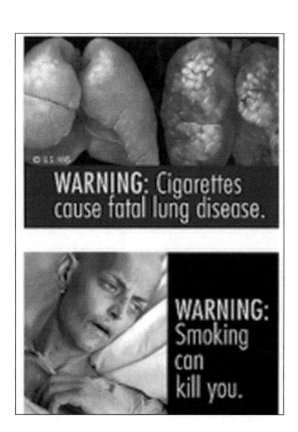

2002: The Tobacco Advertising and Promotion Act aims to wipe out tobacco advertising by 2005, including general advertising, promotions, sponsored events in the UK and sponsorship of global events including Formula 1 and snooker tournaments.

2003: Further EU sanctions made it illegal to brand cigarettes as 'mild' or 'light', and warnings on cigarette packets are enlarged; one covering at least 30% of the packet has to state either 'Smoking Kills' or 'Smoking seriously harms you and others around you'.

2003: The British government invest £31 million in *anti*-smoking campaigns.

2007: It becomes illegal to smoke in public places in the UK such as bars, restaurants and shopping centres and the legal age limit for purchasing tobacco was raised by two years to 18, however the minimum age for possession remained 16

Exercise as a leisure activity was not invented in the last 50 years but the global focus on fitness has undeniably increased. Having a treadmill in your house in 1970 would have been unusual but now it's normal to have equipment at home as well as membership of a local gym or health centre. Both sexes are now expected to keep themselves in shape.

1970s: Fitness, as we know it today, seemed to start with the running boom of the 1970s, primarily a 'jogging' movement in which running was generally pursued alone for recreation and fitness but also a growth in competitive running events in public.

With the advent of the "fun run" the general public suddenly perked up to the joys of running.

Brands like Adidas, Puma, and Nike dominated the running shoe, trainers, market, but every company heard the call for performance-enhancing running shoes. Nike's use of innovative designs and materials ultimately ushered in the arrival of modern-day running shoes.

In the 1970s, workouts were monotonous exercise routines. But all that changed with the advent of the Jazzercise craze. In 1969, dance instructor Judi Sheppard Missett created a dynamic new exercise blending dance, kickboxing, Pilates and yoga. This combination of aerobic exercise and jazz dancing was designed to slim and tone.

114

1980s: High energy aerobic workouts became the fashion and the meteoric rise of home workout videos, led by Jane Fonda, spurred on the popularity of step aerobics. The trend saw millions of people spending good money on small plastic blocks to step on and off repeatedly.

1990s: Mr Motivator, the Jamaican-born British fitness instructor rose to fame through appearances on the UK breakfast television where he performed live fitness sessions and offered tips and advice to viewers. In America, Billy Blanks, a taekwondo instructor, brought Tae Bo to the nation with a combination of taekwondo and boxing.

Roller blading (in line skates) took the place of the 1970s roller skates. There were plenty of gimmicks too. The Shake Weight, a dumbbell with springs attached to the weights, that oscillates in your hand when you jiggle it, alleged to work your upper body more efficiently than a standard dumbbell.

2000s: the decade in which fitness through dance returned. 'Street dance' passed through school yards and local neighbourhoods into dance studios and gyms.

2010: Fast paced Zumba arrived, incorporating elements of hip-hop, salsa, samba, meringue and mambo. Classes, videos and Nintendo games all fuelled the craze. HIIT workouts 'hit' the spot! We've come a long way since the Hula Hoop!

How Attitudes Have Changed

From Corner Shop to Supermarket

There have been major changes to the British diet since the 1970s and by the 21st century, the story of the modern British dinner table is less home cooking, more prepared and takeaway meals; less fish and chips and vastly more meals reflecting our changing culture - more Italian, Indian, SE Asian and North American 'fast food'.

We shop differently. In the 1970s we bought meat at the butcher, fish at the fishmonger, fruit and vegetables at the greengrocer but now 85% of our grocery shopping is at the supermarket and 14% of that is on line. Supermarkets carry a huge range of products including previously unknown salad leaves, spices, exotic fruit and vegetables.

The move towards ever faster food continued. In 1980, the average meal took one hour to prepare. By 1999, that had dropped to 20 minutes. This change was driven by the increasing number of working women and the availability of ready meals. Between 1974 and 2014 "ready meals and convenience meat products" went up five fold.

More people were living on their own, further fuelling the market for fast food. This is matched by a drop in the popularity of fresh, canned and tinned food. The amount of canned peas bought dropped by two thirds between 1974 and 2014. Purchases of white bread have dropped 75% while those of brown and wholemeal bread have risen by 85%. Consumption of eggs peaked in the 1960s and has been declining ever since. Bananas replaced apples as the most popular fruit in 1996. There has been a 30% reduction in fresh vegetables and fruit, we buy many fewer carrots, turnips, parsnips, cabbages and sprouts.

Offal has fallen out of favour among younger, more squeamish Britons. In 1974 a typical household bought 36g of liver per week, but by 2014 the figure had fallen to just 3g - a 92% drop. Pork and mutton also saw more modest falls in popularity, while consumption of uncooked chicken and minced beef rose 62% and 35% over the same period respectively.

TOWARDS OUR FOOD

BURGERS, CHIPS AND PIZZA

Dried and fresh pasta was not even recorded on the National Food Survey until 1998. Between then and 2014, weekly household purchases in this category more than doubled. Pizza rose even more dramatically, with an average purchase from 2g per week in 1975 to 53g in 2014.

The number of takeaway pizzas bought per household shot up 1,000% over the same period. Burgers came to Britain in the 1970s and we eat 2.5 billion beef burgers a year. That roughly works out at the average Brit eating 37 burgers annually. A study of 2,000 adults also found 83% of those who eat meat and fish couldn't 'live' without them.

The nation still loves chips. Sales were three times higher in 2014 than in 1974. However, households reported buying a third less takeaway chips over the same period and the traditional accompaniment has fared differently. In 1974 we bought 44g of white fish - fresh, chilled or frozen - per week and while it is still the most popular fish choice, we buy just 19g a week.

Other types of seafood has done better. Shellfish purchases rose five fold, and those of salmon by 550%.

Consumption of the UK's preferred hot drink, tea, has declined steadily since 1974, from 68g per week to 25g. However, tea remains more popular than instant coffee, cocoa and malted drinks, and the decline has been attributed to "the coffee culture in the UK" and the decline in popularity of sweet biscuits! We drink 12 times as much bottled water now as we did in the 1980s. Skimmed and semi-skimmed milk overtook whole-fat milk in the 1990s and British households now drink four times as much.

HOW ATTITUDES HAVE CHANGED

MORE IS BETTER

'More was certainly better' in the decades following the war and particularly for children. School meals were a way of providing a hot, nutritious meal for every child and free school milk was given out every day to provide all important calcium. In the 1970s, school dinners were 'balanced', typically meat or fish and two veg. Fish and chips with peas or liver and mash with greens, followed by jam roly-poly with custard or rice pudding. Yet this new prosperity was something of a poisoned chalice in relation to the health of the population, obesity was first recognised as a 'hazard to health' in the UK in 1976. Things became worse in 1980 when The Education Act abolished the minimum nutritional standards for school meals and removed the statutory obligation to provide meals for all children.

A 1970s school meal - main course

A 1990s school meal of Turkey Twizzlers, Smiley potato and beans with a sweet dessert

By the 2000s there was a push towards healthier food in schools and turkey twizzlers disappeared from the school canteen, being replaced with options such as fish curry, bean wraps, pasta dishes and salads. However, the trend was still for more and faster food, snacking continued to rise and the intake of fruit and vegetables declined.

The introduction of commercial tendering for school meals resulted in private companies bringing in 'a free-choice, cafeteria system'. The result - the easy option of burgers, chips and chocolate cake. Our children were being fed high calorie, junk food.

A modern day school meal of lasagna, vegetables with fruit and yogurt.

TOWARDS NUTRITION

TOO MUCH CAN BE BAD

As the 21st Century unravels before us, obesity levels are on a meteoric rise. The most obvious explanation for this is that we are a lot less active now than we were in the 70s. We walk a lot less and do less physical work. We snack more and consume a growing number of calories from sugary drinks, crisps and chocolate. We eat more processed foods and ready meals which are still high in sugar and salt. Computers, diet, TV and an 80% reduction in exercise at school, as it no longer holds the importance in the children's week, has contributed to childhood obesity. In the 2010s, the rise of the smartphone had a huge impact on our eating and health habits. Fast food delivery became available literally at our fingertips and online streaming meant we could spend hours on the sofa bingeing on our favourite television shows. During the Covid 19 'lock downs', whilst gyms closed and people worked from home, ordering fast food or cooking lavishly at home became one of the few remaining pleasures to enjoy.

However, we *are* more aware of the issue of obesity and unhealthy lifestyles. Foods carry nutritional information on their packages, salt and sugar content has been reduced in processed food and thanks to public opinion, McDonalds provide salads, 'bottomless' fizzy drinks are no longer the norm and restaurants are obliged to add a calorie count to their menus

Crispy Chicken Salad

1092 kJ | 261 kcal

Freshly prepared salad with chicken breast in a crispy coating, lettuce, cucumber, sliced tomato.

BURGERS

Hamburger
255 Calories
10g Fat
29g Carbs
13g Protein

Cheeseburger
300 Calories
13g Fat
30g Carbs
15g Protein

Double Cheeseburger
410 Calories
21g Fat
30g Carbs
24g Protein

Bacon Cheeseburger
340 Calories
16g Fat
30g Carbs
18g Protein

Bacon Double Cheeseburger
450 Calories
25g Fat
31g Carbs
27g Protein

Whopper Jr.
335 Calories
19g Fat
30g Carbs
15g Protein

The best news is, our average life expectancy is much better than it was. In 1970, the average person was expected to live to 72, while today that has increased to 81.

How Attitudes Have Changed

HOME WORKING

50 years ago, "going to work" meant heading to a physical location outside of your home and working there until 5pm. Today, your spare bedroom or dining room is just as likely to be your office. 43% of workplaces allow employees to work from home at least part of the time. If you DO go to the office, rather than wearing a suit or dress, you are more likely to be wearing jeans and trainers!

COMMUNICATIONS

Back in the 1970s, if you wanted to get in touch – faster than writing a letter and posting it - with a friend, you rang them up on a land-line phone and asked how they were doing. Now, we can see what our friends are up to on their social media. How their relationships are going, where they go on holiday, and, in some cases, what they had for breakfast. Information that used to take time to convey, is now delivered in a second by text or app.

24 HOUR NEWS

Half a century ago, if you wanted to find out what was happening in the world, you'd have to wait for the morning paper to come out. Now the news is on television, websites and apps 24 hours a day. There are hundreds of television channels now, all running day and night. In the 70s the three channels, BBC1, BBC2 and ITV played the National Anthem at midnight and stopped broadcasting. The screens were blank until about six in the morning and of course, no 'catch up' or 'streaming' or 'television whilst you are on the go."

TOWARDS GETTING THINGS DONE

INTERNET SHOPPING

No need now to go to the shop anymore, clothes, music, groceries – anything you can think of – is brought to you with a tap on your computer, tablet or smartphone.

+1 colours/patterns

Outsunny 3 PCs Metal Outdoor Gliding Rocking Chair With Tea Table Patio Garden Comfortable Swing Chair
★★★★☆ ⌄ 8,521

Keter Eden Bench Outdoor Storage Box Garden Furniture, Beige and Brown, 140 x 60 x 84 cm

Garden Corner Sofa rattan Garden Furniture Patio Set Garden Entertaining Set Garden Rattan Furniture...
★★★★☆ ⌄ 27

MEETING AND DATING

Dating 50 years ago meant one of two things. You met someone you liked out in the world and exchanged numbers, or you had someone set you up.

Today, hundreds of potential partners are just a swipe away, thanks to the proliferation of dating apps. Marriage is no longer expected, families are smaller and getting older goes on for longer!

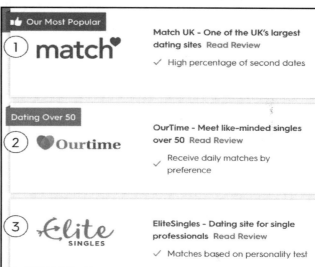

👍 Our Most Popular

1. **match♥**
   Match UK - One of the UK's largest dating sites Read Review
   ✓ High percentage of second dates

Dating Over 50

2. **♥Ourtime**
   OurTime - Meet like-minded singles over 50 Read Review
   ✓ Receive daily matches by preference

3. **Elite SINGLES**
   EliteSingles - Dating site for single professionals Read Review
   ✓ Matches based on personality test

LEISURE

Board games, cards and dominoes have given way to computer games and virtual reality promises travel and other experiences without leaving your sofa! Everyone can watch whatever they want wherever they want on a phone, tablet or computer . You meet and speak with family and friends more via an app than by face to face. We watch more sport,but play less.

1973 Calendar

January

S	M	T	W	T	F	S
	1	2	3	4	5	6
7	8	9	10	11	12	13
14	15	16	17	18	19	20
21	22	23	24	25	26	27
28	29	30	31			

February

S	M	T	W	T	F	S
				1	2	3
4	5	6	7	8	9	10
11	12	13	14	15	16	17
18	19	20	21	22	23	24
25	26	27	28			

March

S	M	T	W	T	F	S
				1	2	3
4	5	6	7	8	9	10
11	12	13	14	15	16	17
18	19	20	21	22	23	24
25	26	27	28	29	30	31

April

S	M	T	W	T	F	S
1	2	3	4	5	6	7
8	9	10	11	12	13	14
15	16	17	18	19	20	21
22	23	24	25	26	27	28
29	30					

May

S	M	T	W	T	F	S
		1	2	3	4	5
6	7	8	9	10	11	12
13	14	15	16	17	18	19
20	21	22	23	24	25	26
27	28	29	30	31		

June

S	M	T	W	T	F	S
					1	2
3	4	5	6	7	8	9
10	11	12	13	14	15	16
17	18	19	20	21	22	23
24	25	26	27	28	29	30

July

S	M	T	W	T	F	S
1	2	3	4	5	6	7
8	9	10	11	12	13	14
15	16	17	18	19	20	21
22	23	24	25	26	27	28
29	30	31				

August

S	M	T	W	T	F	S
			1	2	3	4
5	6	7	8	9	10	11
12	13	14	15	16	17	18
19	20	21	22	23	24	25
26	27	28	29	30	31	

September

S	M	T	W	T	F	S
						1
2	3	4	5	6	7	8
9	10	11	12	13	14	15
16	17	18	19	20	21	22
23	24	25	26	27	28	29
30						

October

S	M	T	W	T	F	S
	1	2	3	4	5	6
7	8	9	10	11	12	13
14	15	16	17	18	19	20
21	22	23	24	25	26	27
28	29	30	31			

November

S	M	T	W	T	F	S
				1	2	3
4	5	6	7	8	9	10
11	12	13	14	15	16	17
18	19	20	21	22	23	24
25	26	27	28	29	30	

December

S	M	T	W	T	F	S
						1
2	3	4	5	6	7	8
9	10	11	12	13	14	15
16	17	18	19	20	21	22
23	24	25	26	27	28	29
30	31					

Printed in Great Britain
by Amazon

28913661R10068